Basics of the Video
Production Diary

OTHER TITLES IN THE SERIES
Basics of Video Production, 2nd edition, Des Lyver and Graham Swainson
Basics of Video Lighting, 2nd edition, Des Lyver and Graham Swainson
Basics of Video Sound, 2nd edition, Des Lyver

FURTHER READING FROM FOCAL PRESS
Film Production Management, 2nd edition, Bastian Cleve
Production Management for Film and Video, 3rd edition, Richard Gates
The Continuity Supervisor, 4th edition, Avril Rowlands
The Essential Television Handbook, Peter Jarvis
Video Production Handbook, 3rd edition, Gerald Millerson

Basics of the Video Production Diary

Des Lyver

Focal Press

OXFORD AUCKLAND BOSTON JOHANNESBURG MELBOURNE NEW DELHI

Focal Press
An imprint of Butterworth-Heinemann
Linacre House, Jordan Hill, Oxford OX2 8DP
225 Wildwood Avenue, Woburn, MA 01801-2041
A division of Reed Educational and Professional Publishing Ltd

  A member of the Reed Elsevier plc group

First published 2001
Transferred to digital printing 2004
© Des Lyver 2001

British Library Cataloguing in Publication Data
A catalogue record for this book is available from the British Library

Library of Congress Cataloging in Publication Data
A catalogue record for this book is available from the Library of Congress

For information on all Focal Press publications visit our website at:
www.focalpress.com

ISBN 0 240 51658 3

Contents

Introduction

This book is aimed at you if you wish to learn about the business side of video production. It is designed to complement the other three in this series (*Basics of Video Production*, *Basics of Video Lighting* and *Basics of Video Sound*), which allow you to understand the overall process of video production and then look in more detail at sound and lighting.

What I have tried to do with this book is to help you with two distinct and different areas of video production. One is to understand the paperwork that will be involved in the production process; the other is to try to heighten your awareness of the communication and business skills you will need if you are intending to set up your own video production company.

We will take a real programme that was made by a real production company. Two people who met on a course like yours, have not been in business long and are struggling to survive, run the company.

Video production requires a high degree of organization to be a success. Good organization will require a proper diary to be kept of your production. It is an understanding of the paperwork, and its organization, that will make your production either a success or a failure.

This book aims to help you produce that paperwork professionally and logically. I have also tried to introduce you to some of the basic principles of setting up and running your own business. For your part, the safety of an educational or training environment will help you to learn from the mistakes we all make in the process of trying to be a success in what is a very tough business.

This is not meant to be an 'expert's book', but if you are a student who wishes to learn about all aspects of planning and documenting a video production, read on.

All types of media productions should have a production diary. Although this book is specifically related to video productions, much of what you read will be directly transferable to film courses, multimedia and sound courses as the basics and principles of running the business remain the same.

The book explains, in simple language, what should go into the diary and how to organize it into a logical order. There are hints and tips to help you avoid the often-costly pitfalls that will beset any new producer who is associated with an expensive production.

You will learn to detail the production process from conceptualization, and how to write the aims and objectives of the programme, right through to the final screening.

My aim is to give you a rapid insight into the process of organizing your video programme without getting bogged down in technical terms. Only where it is necessary to understanding is there any reference to technical matters.

How to use this book

I suggest that you read the first section, explaining what a production diary actually is, before you look at the rest of the book.

It will also make sense if you read the section called 'An outline of our production'. As you will see, if you read this section, the book is based around a simulation of a real production in much the same way as your course will ask you to produce your programme in as real, but safe, an environment as possible.

You may then choose to read this book from cover to cover, but it is essentially designed as a 'dip in' book. You will see that all the different pieces of paper that make up the diary are dealt with separately so it is possible to read only the section that interests you at the moment without reference to the other sections.

This will help you to understand how to deal with the task your course asks you to do today. For example you may have been asked to write a treatment for an imaginary programme. You will find the help you need by looking at the 'treatment' section without necessarily needing to read the whole book. Each section is complete and needs no reference to any other part of the book.

I have spent many years in the video and related AV industry, and have taught video production at all levels. I wrote this text as a result of being unable to find a 'starter book' to offer my students. Thank you for buying it. I hope you find it useful and you have as many happy years in the industry as I have.

Acknowledgements

My sincere thanks are offered to Ace Productions from whom I have borrowed the idea for our imaginary journey through one of their productions from an idea to the final invoice to the client.

I also have to thank Ace Productions' kittens, Chico and Daisy, who already think they are Hollywood stars and tore up most of the paperwork needed for my research!

What is a production diary?

Every programme that is created will generate a great deal of paperwork. All this paperwork needs to be collated and kept in a logical order. The diary starts on the first day a programme is requested and closes on the day the final invoice is paid.

Because it represents the programme from beginning to end it is easier to think of it as a daily record of its life, a diary. Sometimes it is called a production log, sometimes a production file; whatever you have been told to call it I am calling it a production diary and you are going to have to keep one for each production you ever do!

As with any other diary you must get into the habit of putting everything that happens into it, when it happens. It is no good thinking 'boring paperwork' and then trying to remember a phone number or an idea for a credit sequence several weeks later.

The production diary is a complete and accurate record of exactly how that programme was made. It is often seen as your 'insurance policy'; notes relating to meetings, requests for permissions, location details, clearances, every single receipt (including those for sandwiches, pencils and petrol), in fact every single thing that happens during the production process will be there. Any legal or financial query that may arise will be settled by reference to your diary. It stands to reason, therefore, that it must be complete and accurate. The test of a good production diary is that it should allow anyone to completely recreate the programme.

You will have joined a media course because you want to make programmes, that is very understandable and exactly the right reason to be on a course. Unless you intend to make this new skill just an expensive hobby you will realize that part of the making of successful programmes is to make money, to make money you need to be running a business, to run a business you need to be highly organized. All businesses generate paperwork and it is the paperwork as well as the finished product that makes the money.

I have to assume that you are intending to make this venture your career and that is why I am generating paperwork to help you make professional productions!

Why do we need one?

There are many reasons why we have to have a production diary. The prime reason is to log every stage of the production from start to finish. This is necessary so that nothing is missed out or repeated. Time is money. Remember that you only get paid once. If somebody on your team repeats something, or you have to have lengthy meetings to explain to each other what has been done, you will only get paid once. If everything is in the production diary it is a simple matter for the whole team to see exactly the progress of a project, or find an important phone number quickly and easily.

The production diary should allow anyone involved in the production to be able to trace the whole sequence of events, or for a new member of the team to get up to speed quickly and economically. Imagine the cost and potential time wasted if your location manager has all the arrangements for a three-day location shoot in his/her head and then unfortunately has an accident a couple of days before that shoot. You can find a replacement location manager very quickly, but what about the location plans, catering arrangements, contact telephone numbers and so on?

It may be necessary to prove that something was said or done at a later stage in the production. Things can, and do, go wrong. An example would be a security guard agreeing to open a building for you at 8 o'clock in the morning. No one turns up and at 9 o'clock nobody can remember the name of the person, the phone number or who said what. A very expensive crew, cast and tight schedule are now in jeopardy. There is a world of difference between a 'friendly chat with one of the people on site' and the professional formal letter you sent confirming the arrangement that Mr Smith would be available to open the building at 8 o'clock. If the production diary shows to whom the letter was sent, with its reply and the phone numbers, the matter could be resolved very quickly. If you lose time (time is money!) you may be required to produce the evidence of the arrangements in order to claim any compensation.

Often, particularly if money is involved, clients will 'forget' that something was agreed during a meeting. In the enthusiasm of creating a programme lots of ideas are discussed. Often a timid 'well that would cost extra' from you will turn out to be your expense if the client wasn't fully informed, in writing, how much extra and a written confirmation agreeing the extra expense can't be found later.

There are no fixed rules regarding who is responsible for maintaining the diary. In the professional world of large production companies, an administrative team, under the control of the production manager, would look after all the paperwork, smaller companies may make it the responsibility of the PA team. If you are on a production course, part of your course work, and your final mark, will be your production diary. You will have to compile it and present it with your finished programme. Normally it is expected that you will have some help from the rest of your team, but it will be up to you to ensure that it is complete.

What's in it?

There is only one answer to this question – *everything!*

If you look at the contents page of this book you will see that I have listed most of the headings you will use there and the book will run through them one by one. What is important to remember is that wherever possible the documents should be originals. Some of the ideas, phone contacts, notes, etc. may be on scraps of paper, backs of menus, anything. For the sake of neatness and easy access you may, sensibly, type them all out for your diary. Whatever you do, keep the originals, even if it means keeping them separately in another folder. It is the originals that will be required by insurance companies, or courts of law, if a dispute arises. A vital, but often missed, section is the receipts section. In here will go everything that your accountant can cost against the production to save tax. This means doing a petty cash sheet for each week, and attaching the receipts, for things like food, notepads, pencils and of course the ring binder you keep the diary in!

Because the diary will build day by day and it will become your working project document, it is wise to keep it in a ring binder, with dividers for the different sections. You can buy single page pockets to slip the paperwork into and then, if a particular piece is needed, a handy tip is to make sure that the sheet that was taken out is replaced with a note of what it was and who has got it. That way it will always go back in the right place and if someone else needs it, they know where it is.

You will see from the contents page that I have broken my 'diary' into three sections: **pre production**, **production** and **post production**. These are the main production stages. Remember that your diary is designed to make your production go as smoothly as possible. It may be that you have a 'Contacts' section containing all the phone numbers and addresses. Equally you may decide you want a 'Letters' section.

Remember that this is not the boring bit of the course work but the core of the programme that will ensure it goes smoothly, according to plan, on budget, on time and ensures that there are no nasty headaches or problems to get in the way of your creative work.

A good rule to follow is that about 60 to 70 per cent of the total time you spend on the production should be on planning and preparation. Only 30 to 40 per cent is spent on actual production. The more planning and preparation you do the less time you will have to spend on the very expensive production part. The less outgoing expense, the more profit for you!

If you are already thinking that this is all a bit unnecessary, because you already have this great idea for a programme and just want to get the gear out and get on with it, then I have to tell you that you are about to take up a very expensive hobby. Forget about the course, the paperwork and employment in a highly organized and competitive industry and have a lovely time with your camcorder!

How do we organize it?

Your diary should be organized in the way that you find most efficient and convenient. I cannot say to you 'this is the way to do it' because the way you work, and organize things, will not be the same way as I do. I can suggest to you that the easiest 'filing system' is the one that allows you to get on with the job quickly and efficiently. For this reason I suggest you use a ring binder because, as the project develops, the contents will grow and will need to be grouped under different headings in your production diary.

The majority of Production Diaries have three main sections, reflecting the stages of the programme. They will be called 'Pre production', 'Production', and 'Post production'.

Each of these main sections will have divisions for things like 'Contacts', 'Meetings', 'Phone calls' and perhaps 'Notes and ideas'. These will be separate from the divisions for 'Treatment', 'Budget', 'Storyboard', 'Scripts', 'Logs' and so on.

The first page of each division should be an index. How you organise this is crucial. It needs to be simple but, at the same time, allowing instant access to any piece of information contained within the diary. I suggest that every item has a number, perhaps in a circle on the top right hand corner, and the date of origin. It will help if there is also the author's initials on the item somewhere. It is easy to check on something if you know who wrote it!

Let us take a simple example to try to make sense of all of this. We will assume that a letter has arrived from a prospective client, enquiring about a programme they require to be made. Elaine has written some notes, word processed several letters, one to the prospective client, one to a supplier asking for a current rate card and one to a graphic designer. Over a period of time the replies will come back.

On the top right hand corner of the letter from the client we will put '1' and on the bottom right hand corner we will put 'Elaine'. The letter to the supplier will have '2' and 'Elaine', similarly the graphic designer will have '3' and 'Elaine'.

Each of these three letters goes into a separate A4 transparent slip pocket and is put into the section marked 'Letters'.

Our index so far now looks like this:

LETTERS

No.	To/From		Date	Originator
1.	Zena Cook	(F)	09/10/99	Shoe Box Co
2.	TV Supplies	(T)	09/10/99	Elaine
3.	Jim Sandle	(T)	09/10/99	Elaine

Please note that all figures throughout the book represent full A4 pages in your production diary.

You will see that the letters have been numbered from 1 to 3 and the letter received has been identified with an (F) (from) and the name of the person, or with a (T) (to), obviously indicating the letter was sent to, rather than came from. Simple but vital.

The notes that were written before the letters can either be stapled to the relevant letter or kept in a separate (indexed) section marked 'Notes'.

It is important that everything is kept. Notes made at a client meeting, for example, may need to be produced if there is some later dispute about what was actually agreed.

Let us say that Elaine has now replied to the prospective client and also received her rate card and the details she asked the graphic designer for.

These could be labelled 4, 5, and 6, but when you have a whole file full of letters and replies, and have to sort through perhaps 70 or 80 entries, you will wish there was an easier way. The probability is that other letters will be received (and sent) before the graphic designer replies. How are you going to file that if its real number should be 14?

One simple option is to call the letter to the prospective client 1A and file it in the same pocket as the original request. It makes sense to have letter and reply together.

The rate card isn't really a reply to a letter. You may want a separate section called 'Rates and quotes'. How do you deal with that?

One option is to keep a database on your computer to index, and cross reference, everything. You may even decide to use a scanner and keep everything on the computer. You should still have all the originals filed in a production diary as back up. It isn't a question of 'if the computer crashes' but 'when it crashes'!

Your index page may now look like this:

				LETTERS	
No.	To/From		Date	Originator	
1.	Zena Cook	(F)	09/10/99	Shoe Box Co	
2.	TV Supplies	(T)	09/10/99	Elaine	
3.	Jim Sandle	(T)	09/10/99	Elaine	
1A	Zena Cook	(T)	14/10/99	Elaine	
2.	TV Supplies	(F)	16/10/99	R & Q 1.	
3A	Elaine	(T)	21/10/99	Jim Sandle	
4.	MCPS	(T)	22/10/99	Simon	

You will see that the rate card is referenced as 2, which will lead you to the request letter, and has been placed in a separate section (Rates and quotes) as 1.

There is also another letter in the file. Simon has written to MCPS to ask for their current rate card.

It may be that you now need to open a new section called 'Contacts'. Already you have several names, addresses and phone numbers which may be easier to find quickly in an 'address book' style section.

This is a simple, but limited, example of organization. It may be that nothing further happens about the prospective client and programme, in which case the programme file is closed and filed. Never throw anything away, one day you will need to refer back to it!

Of course the hope is that this will develop into a real programme and real work. The idea of keeping separate sections, with indexes that can be cross referenced, now makes even more sense and becomes more important.

You may choose to use a database to organize all the paperwork relevant to the programme into a series of fields that will allow you to do detailed searches. Whilst this is undoubtedly quicker you must still keep all the original paperwork in separate sections of a folder.

As the programme builds, and the paper mountain grows, make regular back up copies, and a hard copy of all your work. Never rely on 'automatic time saved back ups'. Computers can be absolutely guaranteed to crash at the most inconvenient moment.

An outline of our production

To make this book as real as possible I have borrowed a production made by Ace Productions. It is typical of the sort of productions you will do for your course. During your course, or when you are just starting out in business, you will need to know a little about business procedures. What follows is a realistic overview of life in a small production company and how they go about getting work. There are lots of ideas included that will help you to understand how you need to start.

Ace Productions is a small company that specializes in short corporate style programmes for a range of small to medium sized companies and some public sector organizations. Two people run it. Elaine is the programme producer and director. She works with Simon, who acts as production manager and PA. At the moment they do not employ anybody directly and work from a small office that has two rooms. One is the 'front office' where meetings with clients, crew and performers take place. The paperwork and general running of the company also take place in this room. The other room is the 'engine room'. In here is a VHS edit suite, a small computer graphics facility, and a few odd bits of equipment like a Hi8 recorder, a Polaroid camera, a portable mini disc recorder, a few very basic lights and a photocopier.

They decided on the VHS edit suite because VHS is still the most common replay system in homes and offices and they find it helpful to give clients copies of ideas, rough cuts of the programme and so on. They also know that they can have a VHS copy of anything they may shoot made very cheaply. They do rough cut edits here to see how the programme is going together. They have used it for off line editing (using burnt in time code) for low budget productions.

Elaine deals with the clients and she will often direct the programme, having written the script. Simon looks after the locations, organizes a studio, books the crew and cast, keeps all the programme notes and logs and in all other ways manages the production.

Around them they have a team of freelance people who do the camera work, sound, lighting and editing. Elaine and Simon find it cheaper for a small production company to buy in these experts for each production because, as specialists in their field, they either have, or can provide the right type of equipment for each programme. These freelancers have all worked together and have formed a real crew spirit with Elaine and Simon.

Both Elaine and Simon have spent time on sending out direct mail shots to their chosen client base and have built up a reputation for being able to provide very professional programmes within budget and on time. Today a letter has arrived from Pat Hermandes, who is a projects officer with a company called Fashions for You, asking Ace Productions to make contact regarding a short video they need shooting to highlight the care that goes into the making of their clothes. They will run this video on their stand at trade shows, to attract more retail outlets to stock their range of casual clothing for young adults.

Elaine and Simon read the letter and decide that this is the sort of programme they can handle. This single sheet of paper is all that is needed to start the whole ball rolling towards another successful Ace Productions programme. Elaine and Simon know that it is more than possible that other companies will have got the same letter and there is no certainty that they will be given the contract to produce the video. They realize that their initial reply will be crucial in securing the contract.

This then is the scenario for the rest of this book. You will see how Elaine and Simon deal with everything from this first contact to the final hand over of the programme. Remember that this is not a book about how to produce a video; others in this 'basics' series deal with that aspect. Here we are only concerned with the paperwork that goes with a programme.

Pre production

The pre production stage is the first stage of any programme. This is when the planning and preparation that is needed to actually make the programme is done.

Pre production is very important and will usually take up nearly three quarters of the total time between getting a request to make a programme and its final delivery to the client.

This is the time that will need all your communication and management skills. Apart from designing and writing the programme you will have to meet people, negotiate with them, look after them, plan every last detail of the actual shooting and editing and be able to work out budgets and costs so that you offer a fair product for a fair price and make a fair profit.

Every time you go through this process it will get easier and more familiar. Your course will probably allow for this by asking you to write treatments, storyboards, scripts and so on as you practice making programmes. Eventually you will have to go to a client, take the brief and do all the planning yourself.

There are people in the industry who find this side of a production so absorbing and challenging that they make it their career. They are production managers and producers. They are responsible for the production rather than the shooting of it, which is left to the director and crew.

If you eventually intend to start your own production company you will need to become very skilled in this area, or be prepared to employ someone who is, unless you are going to produce small scale corporate type programmes which you can produce and direct. Two important jobs does mean two workloads but won't necessarily mean two salaries!

If you have read the section called 'An outline of our production' you will see that two people run Ace Productions. Elaine looks after the clients and writes and directs the programme, while Simon looks after the management side and is responsible for bookings, logs and locations. It is one of their programmes that we will now follow.

There is no one way that a request for a programme will arrive. You could receive a phone call, a letter or fax, a personal approach or you could reply to a tender request in a trade paper. We will look at examples of phone and letter requests.

The request for a programme – by phone

Phone calls are probably the most difficult to deal with because you will have to think on your feet, take notes, be very careful what you say and sound professional all at the same time.

Imagine this telephone conversation and see how many mistakes you can spot.

The phone rings and you pick it up:

'Hello'

'Is that Telly Productions?'

'Yeah. Who wants to know?'

'This is Jean Bright, marketing manager of Toys for All; we are looking for a promotional video. Is that the sort of thing you do?'

'Yeah, all the time, and we won't charge you an arm and a leg.'

'Could we meet and discuss some details and prices?'

'We're pretty busy at the moment but if you want to pop in sometime tomorrow I can probably spare a couple of minutes. Or, better still, I am always in the Rose and Crown for lunch so I could see you there and buy you a beer.'

'I have got a busy schedule at the moment, and some other phone calls to make, so perhaps I will ring you back.'

'OK but make it first thing in the morning next time.'

You are right. Jean Bright did not ring back, or go to the Rose and Crown, and Telly Productions are still looking for their first job.

Often the really silly examples are the best because you know you wouldn't respond like that. But what about the mistakes?

Always answer the phone in a professional manner. The company and your name should be part of the response. *Telly Productions, Pat speaking, how can I help?'* suggests a professional organization. This is a very important first contact.

Be honest. If you have done a promotional video before say so, but do not 'name drop', clients are looking for confidentiality and to be told that you have done a promotional video for their biggest rival is not going to help. A simple *'Yes we have done promotional videos for other organizations'* is enough. If you haven't, don't say *'No never, but we are always willing to give it a try'*. Far better to say *'We have done similar programmes, yes'*.

Don't ever refer to the cost, even if asked. You cannot put a price on a programme you know nothing about. Only if asked directly be honest and professional. *'It would be unfair to both of us to put a price on anything until we have discussed your exact requirements. You will, however find our prices very competitive.'*

If you are asked to meet and discuss it, there are two ways of dealing with this. Neither is right or wrong, just different. The first way involves you saying something like *'Let's get our diaries together, have you got a preferred day?'* Having sorted out a mutually convenient day the next problem is to sort out where. This is not as straightforward as it might appear. If, for example, you are working in your back bedroom, you hardly want clients there on a first visit do you? If you have an office, offer it as a second choice, so it is either *'Could you warn security that I will be coming to see you?'* or *'Shall I come to you or would you prefer to see our facilities here?'*

The second way is arguably more professional and probably more time constructive. Don't arrange to meet until you have something to discuss. How about *'Perhaps it would be more constructive if you could send me some details of what you have in mind, then we could arrange to meet and discuss them?'* If you have even a rough idea of what is wanted it will be easier to guess a price range if asked.

Always ask for an address and contact number and remember to say thank you. So *'Thank you for calling us. Could I take an address and contact phone number, please?'* will end your professional call and you will know that the potential client already has a positive image of your company. This is very important because, even if you do not get this job, Jean Bright might be impressed enough to offer your name to other potential clients that she talks to.

One final important point: you spend a lot of money on advertising to get the work in the first place. It is very helpful to know which adverts work and which don't. Always ask how clients heard of you. Again there are no fixed rules about when you ask. The rule is ask nicely, 'How did you get our number then?' just won't do! *'May I ask how you found out about us?'* is about right.

All of this conversation, with names, addresses and any details must be written down. It is the first page of your production diary, under the heading 'Requests for programmes.' Even if you never hear any more from Jean Bright, she, and her company, are a useful contact when you send out your next mail shot.

The request for a programme – by letter

Look at this letter that has been received from Fashions for You. The first thing is to read it more than once so that you understand it, then ask some questions: What is it asking for? Is it a request for information? What information? Is it a request for a programme to be made? Is it a request for a meeting? How are you going to reply? By letter or phone?

The list of questions is almost endless. Two things depend on how you answer this letter. One is whether we get a programme to make, the other is whether I can write the rest of this book because this is the letter that Ace Productions got and upon which this book is based. Fashions for You and Ace Productions are relying on you!

What we need to do is learn as much as possible about what is being asked and, perhaps more important, what we are not being told. Let's look at the letter in some detail and answer some of the questions. First look at the company logo. Under the name is something called their USP or KSP, this stands for unique selling point or key selling point: *'exciting, affordable clothing for you'* is their identity of themselves. This is important to you because the programme will have to reflect this.

FASHIONS FOR YOU
exciting, affordable clothing for you

21, Gothic Road
Genie Town
GT64 2TX

Telephone: 96795 376281   *Fax: 96795 397401*

Ace Productions
39 West Street
Genie Town GT64 6DE

8th July 1999

Dear Elaine Booker,

We have kept the brochure you sent us on file for some time. We are now looking to commission a short video for use on our stand at trade shows and would be interested to hear your ideas on producing it.

Fashions for You is a medium-sized company selling direct to specialized retail outlets. We produce a range of smart casual wear for both sexes in the late teen, early twenty age bracket. We are proud of our designs and the quality of production.

The Sales Department has suggested that static images in a brochure cannot convey the whole ethos of our product. They feel that a video running continuously on our Trade Stand would serve the two purposes of attracting more buyers to the stand, whilst being able to show them the quality of manufacture.

It may be that some of our customers would like to use the video as a 'retail presenter' in their stores and we would like to explore this option.

We would welcome your comments together with an indication regarding possible costs and the time involved.

Yours sincerely,

Pat Hermandes

Pat Hermandes

Projects Officer

They don't sell 'ordinary' or 'normal' clothing; they sell 'exciting, affordable' clothing.

Business is about having an identity that makes you stand out from the competition. You will do well to remember exciting and affordable because you will drop these words into conversations with this client at meetings and use them in their programme.

It may be that your course requires you to invent your own company to make your programmes and files more realistic. Give some thought to your logo and USP. Ace Productions' USP is 'Video Programmes on Budget & on Time' and you will see it on their paperwork. It is their identity that separates them from 'normal' companies.

The first paragraph is an important answer to the question 'how did you hear of us?', it is also a warning. They kept the brochure you sent them. You should keep a note somewhere in your business files showing who you sent mail shots to, when or whether they replied.

Why is it a warning? Think about it, if they kept yours they must have a file of 'Production companies'. Most companies do, very few use telephone directories. You are not the only video producer in the world; other companies will have got this letter too. This would be normal. What you do next, with your reply, will determine whether you get a meeting. What you do at that meeting will determine whether you get the programme.

The next sentence shows this is a real enquiry, there will be a programme made. They have thought about it and this means they already have an idea about the content. They are intending to 'commission a short video for use at trade shows'.

The second paragraph tells you who they are, what they do and whom they sell to. It also has another selling point you will use in the programme: they are proud of their designs and quality of productions. This is not a company that produces either rubbish or designer wear, but they do have exciting affordable, quality goods.

The third paragraph tells us how they see the video. This is not going to be a collection of static images; their brochure obviously does that. It wants excitement and movement. It must stop people walking past their stand. It is a sales facilitator type of programme. That means we make a programme showing exciting, affordable, quality clothing designed for the young adult of today, get people to stop and watch it, and then their sales people sell.

The fourth paragraph is not as simple as it seems. The company has obviously seen videos on other trade stands and they have also seen product videos in stores. These two videos are different types, aiming at different audiences. What works for one audience will not necessarily work for another. A compromise won't work for either. What this paragraph says is that they want the video primarily for their stand, but they would like to explore the possibility of extending it to another audience. They don't know how it can be done and want to explore the possibility with you. It is a trap. How you deal with this sort of innocent wording is crucial. It will come up again later in the book, so for the moment we will just store it away in our heads.

Our reply to the last paragraph will be the key to getting, or losing, the programme. Do not be tempted to write back and say *'we do programmes like this all the time. It will be £5000 and will take a week'.*

They have asked for an indication of price and time. We cannot do the programme until we have a full brief, we cannot cost it until we know what is involved; what if you find out later that their factory is in the Far East and it will take a week to shoot with six crew? There would not be much left of your £5000, or your week to produce, then would there? This requires some thought and is another trap. We will have to think of something that does not commit us, but does not lose us the programme.

Finally look at the person who sent the letter. Is Pat Hermandes male or female? Does it matter? It would if you decide to reply by phone and ask to speak to Mr Hermandes, only to be told 'this is Miss Hermandes speaking'.

Look at the job title. What is a projects officer? Not a project manager. Not a marketing manager. Is this someone in an office who has been told to investigate the possibility of a video? Is Pat in charge of the budget? Can Pat make decisions? Is Pat even the client?

At this stage it doesn't matter. Pat is our only contact. Later, if we get the commission, we will have to find out how much authority Pat actually has. We cannot have a situation where we need a decision now and are then told by Pat Hermandes that it will have to be referred to the procurement committee, which meets once a month.

Finally, we have spent a lot of time looking at, thinking about and developing this letter. All the thoughts, and questions, should have been noted down. Remember that everything goes into the production diary. We will need these immediate thoughts about what this letter says to form part of our reply. We should have not only the letter, but also our thoughts on paper beside us when we compose our reply.

Before we can reply, we need to think about the aims and objectives of this programme.

Aims

It is important to remember that a television programme is an audio and visual experience. This means that the whole thing must be thought out in both sound and picture. Programmes will not work if either is thought of in isolation. It is never a success to try and fit sound to existing pictures or pictures to existing sound. The only exception to this is possibly the pop video where the song exists first, and then pictures are fitted to reflect the mood or theme of the song. Sometimes this works reasonably well, but attempting it is a specialist skill.

The programme must have some sort of aim, without an aim the programme will wander 'aimlessly'. The aim is an initial idea, often quite vague in nature, along the lines of, for instance, 'we will do a programme on fashion'. The importance of an aim is that it gives something to focus on, a starting point, we now know the programme will concern itself with promoting stylish clothing. This germ of an idea gives us the concept of the programme that can be stated as an aim, 'We will do something to promote this range of exciting, affordable, quality clothing'.

Objectives

The next stage is to write down some objectives; these are precise statements of intent. To take our example, fashion is so vast a subject that we need to select an area or areas that the programme will concentrate on. We need to set time limits for the programme. We need to define the type of programme, is this a serious documentary or a comedy for instance. Above all we need to define the content. Most of the answers to this question can be found, often hidden, in the letter requesting a programme.

Sometimes you will get a request with the aim and objective clearly stated. More often you will have to work it out, as in this case, from the information you have been given in the request and then from subsequent meetings with the client. We might end up with a statement such as 'We will do a short (5–7 minute) promotional programme, promoting the "Fashions for You" range of clothing to buyers visiting their trade stand. The programme has the objective of stopping passing trade and assisting the sales department in increasing their output to retail stores.'

From our idea, or aim, we have now moved to a much more precise statement of what the programme is about. The precision of our objective is such that it is measurable. This means that we can test whether the programme met its objective. Did our programme stop people walking past the Fashions for You stand? As a result of watching the programme did their retail sales increase? Only if we have an objective and we test it through the results of the programme can we really say whether the programme was a success or not.

The certainty is that the client has an objective in mind. Your difficulty is making sure that both of you are working on the same objective and that the objective is met. Difficulties will arise with final payment to you if the client does not think the programme meets their objective. It is crucial, therefore that both of you agree an objective, preferably in writing, and that the objective is referred to throughout the production to ensure that it is met by the picture and sound track content.

Target audience

At this early stage we need to define whom this programme is aimed at. The whole structure of the programme and its language and images must be fitted around a particular group of people. If a programme is intended for children, for instance, the visual and aural language will be much simpler than if the programme was aimed at university professors. Defining the target audience will keep our minds on who we are making the programme for. In our example we are trying to heighten awareness within a particular group of people – retail buyers at a trade fair – of the existence of, and sense in buying, Fashions for You clothing. This a specialist programme with a very limited target audience.

Both the objective and the target audience really go together and need thinking about together. If the two are too rigorously structured it becomes easy to lose any creativity that may be brought to the programme. A simple approach is to start off by thinking about what we want to do and to whom. This can then be tightened up at a later stage. The really important thing is that if we have precise objectives and target audience we can avoid the traps.

This programme's objectives and target audience are not the same as a programme that would attract customers in the shops to buy a particular range of clothing. We cannot have one programme for two conflicting uses; therefore we need two programmes, or a modification of one.

Don't forget, all of these aims, objectives and target audience notes go in the production diary with a heading at the top of the page *'Fashions for You – (and the date)'*.

You might find it helpful to write down what you think are the aims, objectives and target audience based on the request letter. It will help you to focus your mind on your reply and on your production of this programme. There is no reason why you should accept my suggestions. The important thing is that you understand the principles. I suggest that when you have done that, you reply to Pat Hermandes before you go on to look at Ace Productions' reply. You will then be able to compare them and see how much you have learnt so far.

The reply

There is one main purpose to our reply. We want the programme! What we need to do is to pick up on as much of the request as possible (which is why we spent so long looking at it and writing notes), be professional, sell our services and appear approachable.

Above all you need to be honest. If you are not, you will be caught out sooner or later. If this is the sort of programme you cannot do, don't want to do, or don't have the time to do, say so as tactfully as possible. A simple *'Thank you for your enquiry about a video. We do not do this type of video and it would, therefore, be unfair to suggest that we do.'* or, *'We would enjoy working with you on your video but unfortunately we could not meet realistic deadlines at the moment due to the pressure of work'* is enough.

Similarly do not give too much away. The idea of a reply is to say 'yes we are interested', not to explain in great detail how you would do it. You do need to put in enough for the client to want to know more, but not so much that your whole idea is given to another company as the client's idea.

Look at Ace Productions' reply, and compare it with your own. We will take a little time to work out what has been said.

Ace Productions
Video Programmes on Budget & on Time

39, West Street
Genie Town
GT64 6DE

Tel: 96795 230871
Fax: 96795 230858

Fashions for You
21 Gothic Road
Genie Town GT64 2TX

9th July 1999

Dear Pat Hermandes,

Thank you for your letter regarding your commission for a short video for use on your trade stands. We are very interested in producing this exciting venture.

I have to agree that your casual shirts, in particular, are very good value and tell you that the two I have are the envy of my friends!

We would see this video as reflecting the vibrancy of youth, through its soundtrack, and would be aimed at stopping potential customers from passing your stand. The visuals would consist of real people wearing your designs. We totally agree that static images can only do so much. We would see this programme being interspersed with shots of your designers at work and the production process. This would not only give continuity to the programme but also allow for passing trade to have continuously changing images forming short stories in their own right.

The retail presenter idea is a natural progression and we should discuss ways of incorporating that into the programme.

Regarding costs and time, we pride ourselves in being able to produce professional videos on budget and on time. You will find our prices very competitive, but it would be unfair on both of us to suggest a figure before we decide on a programme outline.

We do not charge for any of the initial development work and would be glad of an opportunity to discuss this exciting project with you further.

I look forward to hearing from you when we can, hopefully, get our diaries together.

Yours sincerely,

Elaine Booker

Elaine Booker

Producer

The most important thing with a reply is its length. A short note saying 'yes we are interested' won't do and neither will several pages on the life and times of you and your company. A guide is to keep it to one side of paper while answering all the points in their letter.

First of all notice that Ace Productions has addressed the letter 'Dear Pat Hermandes'. This is for two reasons; the first is that is the way the letter was signed. The second is that it gets them out of the awkward situation of is Pat male or female. It would be quite wrong to become too friendly too soon and write 'Dear Pat', it would be a mistake to guess and put 'Dear Ms' or 'Dear Mr', and I am sure you wouldn't dream of 'Dear Sir or Madam'!

The first paragraph is the standard 'Thank you for considering us' opening. Notice, though, that apart from saying we are interested, the Fashions for You key selling point has been picked up by saying 'this exciting venture'.

The second paragraph shows two things, both very subtle. Elaine has done some research into their products and has found a clever way of saying that she is in the age group of people they are trying to sell to. This means that she will be able to identify with the product much more easily than say a middle aged male. It is not essential that this sort of thing is put in, but with lots of companies being considered it may swing things in your favour if they feel you are already familiar with the product.

The third paragraph is the longest and the one that is the most important. Fashions for You want a programme to show on their trade stand. This means that there will be a passing trade that needs to be stopped from passing. There is a possibility that all, or parts, of the programme will be used in stores to attract the youth of today. The Sales Department see a problem with static brochures. We want to do this programme and need to offer enough of a carrot to be asked more. This paragraph has not said what the programme actually looks like but it has said how we see the programme idea developing. Remember to make it just enough for them to bite. Don't give long explanations and creative ideas that can be stolen and given to another production company.

Look at how we have guided them around using the same programme for the retail presenter. The problem with using the programme for two purposes is that there are two target audiences and two separate objectives (as mentioned earlier). We would like to do two programmes, and get more money, so it is sensible to leave this as 'we should discuss it'.

Notice that the subject of cost is also skirted around. This is a standard trick, they know what their budget is, you know roughly what the programme will cost and want all the budget! Ace Productions have used their USP (Video Programmes on Budget & on Time), and at the same time shown honesty by saying 'it would be unfair on both of us (yet)'.

It is standard practice to not charge for initial development work (meetings, phone calls etc.). This cost can always be hidden in the programme fee should you get the commission.

It is sensible to use the last line. The client is placed under an obligation to reply. Hopefully there are enough of the three important ingredients in our reply for us to be given the job.

What are the three important ingredients? One is to show interest in, and preferably knowledge of, the product. One is to give enough of an outline for the programme for them to want to know more. One is to appear honest and professional.

If you took the time to write your own reply before reading Ace Productions' reply, and this explanation, it would be worth looking for those three ingredients in your response.

Remember that there is no standard letter of reply. Yours is probably as good, if not better, than Ace Productions'. Your programme idea will not be the same. The client will decide what is best suited to their needs from all the replies.

Client meeting – preparation

We will assume that a week or ten days has passed. You haven't heard from Pat Hermandes and wonder what to do next. It is not wise to telephone, either the letter has arrived or it hasn't. If you wanted to know if it had arrived you would, presumably, have registered it and then you could have asked the Post Office. If it has arrived it has presumably been read. Decisions will now have to be taken. Maybe there are five or six letters from other companies about the same programme. It is quite possible that two or three contain good ideas and the client is now holding meetings to decide what to do next.

A good habit to get into is for you to image you are the client. Read your letter of reply as if you were the client. Be honest, is there enough in it to make you want to see this producer? Read Ace Productions' reply; would you like to see them?

Out of courtesy you will normally get a reply. It may not be the one you wanted, but you will get it. Do not forget to keep everything. You should have a file for requests, replies and rejections. These are business files, not production files, they will form part of your mailing list and the more requests you get, and the more replies you send, the more experienced you will become.

Just when you begin to think that the rejection letter will come today, the phone rings.

You answer it in a professional manner stating the company name and your name; never just say 'hello'. It is Pat Hermandes' secretary.

She says that Mr Hermandes would like to arrange a meeting to discuss the proposed video. Did you notice the crucial point the secretary has just made? The mystery of Pat Hermandes is solved – he is a man! This could affect the way that you now deal with this client.

You reply with ' I've got my diary in front of me' (you have haven't you!). You ask when would be convenient. If the time suggested is not convenient, say so. Honesty is the best policy and it is normal to have to move meetings around or change dates. It is simple to say that Wednesday afternoon is a bit awkward, but if that is the only time he has you could move things around.

Always remember to ask all the questions you need to; it is not professional to keep ringing back. Is this meeting at Fashions for You or is Mr Hermandes coming to you? If you are driving do you need to know if you can park, are you confident enough to assume there is visitor parking or will you rely on a convenient double yellow line? How long will this initial meeting be? Do you know where you are going? A simple *'That will be at 21 Gothic Road, will it? Do you have any visitor parking?'* gets you out of 'your place or mine' and the worry of parking.

Having arranged this meeting there are now two things you can do. Neither is right or wrong, it comes down to how you feel about it. This is a new development in the programme planning so something needs to go in the production diary. Either write a note, with the date on top, saying that Mr Hermandes' secretary rang to arrange a meeting for Tuesday 20th July at 2 p.m. at Fashions for You which is expected to last for half an hour, or write a letter to Mr Hermandes confirming the arrangements. A copy of this letter will then go in the production diary.

This first meeting is crucial. You have not yet got the programme. The sensible way of looking at this meeting is to imagine it is a job interview. What you may find helpful, at this stage, is to write down what you will do before the meeting, what you will take to the meeting, what questions you think you will be asked and what questions you will ask. Then go on to read how Elaine Booker, of Ace Productions, handled it.

Pre meeting planning

You will remember that Elaine Booker deals with the clients for Ace Productions and wrote the reply we looked at that resulted in her getting an initial meeting with Pat Hermandes. You will find it helpful to compare the way you would handle the preparation for this meeting with the way she did.

The first thing Elaine did was to go to the production diary and remind herself of what Pat Hermandes had said in the request letter, and what she had said in reply. She did this because it helped put her in the right frame of mind to concentrate on the company and the outline of the programme.

Elaine understands that the better she knows the company's product, the easier it will be to talk to Pat Hermandes about it and how the programme might go. She needs to do a little research. She goes to the local store that sells the Fashions for You designs and looks at them. Are they fashionable? What does the range consist of? What is the quality of manufacture? Are they affordable? How does the assistant describe them? Are they comfortable? Could she be seen in them? Does the range change with the seasons?

At the same time she is thinking about the programme. The opening shot is important, but what is the opening shot? This is a video that has no end or beginning because it will be on a trade stand and people will pick it up as they go past. It is going to be more of a series of connected adverts.

She goes back to the office and writes up her notes. From the notes comes a series of unanswered questions. Where is the factory? Who are the designers? How can she show the clothes in an exciting way, particularly if they are not? All these notes go into the production diary.

Having researched the product, she tries to work out the questions she will be asked. It helps to have someone to work on this with, so now is the time to involve her partner at Ace Productions, Simon. They look at her reply letter again.

'Tell me how you see this programme developing?' is an obvious question. They think about the soundtrack that is going to reflect the 'vibrancy of youth'. This will be punchy, modern music. There will be very few words; she cannot tell a story because of the nature of the programme that has no end and no beginning. An idea develops from her original reply; they will show the designs from designer through manufacture to a catwalk display and on to the retail outlet. Each section will be short and the order that the viewer sees them is irrelevant. All the stages are there; all will stand up on their own and link from the stage behind to the stage in front.

'How do we get over the seasonal changes?' Simon suggests that they simply replace the catwalk section. This would not be expensive, but would mean that they get to work with Fashions for You on a regular basis.

'What about the video presenter?' A change of emphasis to the voice track highlighting the benefit to the customer, an additional scene of real people wearing the designs in real situations. A natural 'tweak' to an existing programme. Again, not expensive but ensuring a continuity of work with Fashions for You.

'Cost?' Difficult. Simon knows how much it costs to hire a crew on a day rate basis, knows how much editing costs and knows how much Ace Productions want for the development work. He can guess at how long this programme will take. What he does not know is the budget. Simon also knows that any programme can be made cheaply or, with extra refinements, clever effects and editing, can cost a great deal more. They decide that Elaine will say what she has always said *'That depends on the quality you require. A basic programme would be around £10,000 but using famous actors or complicated effects would add to that. The sensible thing for us to do is see what we can get into your budget.'*

All these thoughts and notes are written up and put in the production diary, perhaps in a new section called Research and Development.

You will begin to see that a very large part of production relies on communication skills, attitude and teamwork. A good course will teach you these skills. Even if you eventually decide that you only want to be a camera person, or an editor, you will still need these skills to communicate and negotiate with your team and all the other people involved in the production.

Client meeting – the meeting

You have done as much preparation as you can and now you go to the meeting. Remember you are going as a salesperson whose job is to sell yourself as honest, efficient and knowledgeable as well as someone who sells video productions. It is very important that you are in the right frame of mind. Often with this stage of the course your 'client' will be your course tutor or another lecturer that you already know. This does not matter because you are in a role play situation and you both pretend that you are somebody else. Elaine and Simon have made all the mistakes during their course and, having now completed the course, have set up in business.

You turn up for the meeting representing your company, prepared to be interviewed for a job. You will have a folder containing a copy of the original request and your reply, your notes and thoughts about the programme idea and a notebook to make more notes based on what you and Mr Hermandes discuss.

It is sensible to aim to allow lots of time to get to the meeting. Things happen that are out of your control, trains don't run, cars break down, car parks are full. To be early leaves you stress free and perhaps with enough time for a cup of coffee before your meeting. You would not be the first producer to arrive late only to find the client cannot now see you because he is in another meeting, probably with another producer who has arrived on time!

We will sit in on Elaine's meeting with Mr Hermandes and see how she does. It will be helpful for you to imagine you are Elaine and think how you would answer the questions.

There are a couple of minutes 'pleasantries' of introduction, and then Mr Hermandes picks up Elaine's reply from his desk. Elaine opens her folder and gets her notebook out.

'Apart from thinking that this video will be between 5 and 10 minutes long and wanting to emphasize the quality of manufacture, as well as our range of clothing, we are open to ideas and suggestions. I like your idea of the soundtrack reflecting the vibrancy of youth, can you tell me more about the way you see this happening?'

As he is talking Elaine writes 5–10 minutes run time in her notebook. 'Well, we thought of using a punchy non-vocal track to link a series of images together. It would be rather like a pop video, the music makes you want to stop and watch, the images tell the story.'

'Wouldn't that be rather expensive? Surely you can't just take a piece of pop music and use it as a sound track for our video?'

'No we wouldn't suggest the expense of using a popular tune. There are music libraries we can use that produce similar tracks and are very reasonable to licence for non broadcast applications, such as this. We also have a supplier who will write and perform something appropriate especially for your programme at an acceptable price.'

Elaine makes a note to contact Julian, a friend of Simon who often helps out with their sound tracks with the help of his synthesizer.

'Your idea of the visuals seems a little uncoordinated. We had thought of a story following the range from designer, through manufacture to wearer, can you explain how you will show that continuity?'

'We need to look at the situation realistically. Imagine you are at a trade fair, walking around the stands. You hear a punchy soundtrack and move towards the Fashions for You stand. It is very unlikely that you will arrive as the opening credits are showing and stay for the whole 10 minutes watching a story. It is more likely that the programme will be some minutes in, hopefully the soundtrack will attract you for a minute, allowing the Fashions for You sales people time to approach you. During the minute or so you have been watching you have seen cameos of the design, manufacture and range. In that way the continuity is in the cameos, rather like an advertisement.'

'But we don't want static images.'

'No, our idea is to show the designers working, and use fairly close shots to show the quality of manufacturing, the quality of the stitching for example. The clothes themselves, we thought, would be worn and paraded as a catwalk show, with exciting lighting and camera angles.'

'I like that idea, but how much are we talking about to get models and catwalks?'

Elaine makes a note that he has a very limited budget, that is twice he has said that sounds expensive!

'We pride ourselves on being able to produce the best programme possible and keep within budget. If your budget cannot stretch to professional models, then there are other ways. We have, for instance, a very strong working relationship with the local dance and drama college.'

'A catwalk would be easy to construct in a studio with proper lighting and all the modelling sections could be shot in a day.' Another note in Elaine's notebook to remind her to contact the local college and see if they would be interested.

'Let's look at the retail presenter use. Sales are very keen that we should get the most use out of this programme. Do I get the impression that you cannot produce a programme that fits both roles?' Elaine had guessed that this question would come up in some form, so her answer was ready. 'What we feel is that there are two different target audiences. One is trade buyers, probably wholesalers and retail purchases managers, and the other is people like me, who go into the shop and need to be persuaded to buy your clothes and not someone else's! There are two different needs. What I am suggesting is that we can use the same images but edited differently to tell the right story for each type of viewer. It is more likely, for instance, that the person in the shop would be there for long enough to see a story. We could produce two programmes consisting of material shot for one, but edited differently, so I cannot see it costing much more.'

Mr Hermandes likes that idea, but says he will have to discuss it with sales so the two of them will need to discuss it further after that. Elaine is sufficiently experienced to note two things – see if you spotted them. One is that he is probably not the client. It must be discussed with sales. Sales have the budget and final say. The second is perhaps more important, he likes the whole idea; he has let slip that he likes the idea and is thinking of another meeting (will need to discuss it further).

'Have we got enough information to discuss price and time scale?' Elaine was waiting for this. She has to answer because another producer may be the next meeting and may have decided on a price. She starts with time scale. 'The programme production time is critical to cost. We will need access to your designers, your factory and your range of clothing. I think you liked the idea of models wearing the clothing so we will need to set up studio time.' Mr Hermandes interrupts with the fact that the designers are in this building and the factory is only 20 minutes away in the car. He agrees that he does like the models idea and the vibrant, punchy music. He also lets slip that he can almost see and feel the video, which sounds very good. Elaine has to risk it. 'Can I know what your budget is, then I can work some figures out and cost it out for you within the week?' This is a very fair way of proceeding at this stage. It is honest and does not need further explanation. Mr Hermandes suggests that they are thinking it will cost 'in the region of £8000'. He agrees that it will be helpful if Elaine sends him a treatment and cost breakdown within a week. He adds that time is important because the first trade fair is only a couple of months away.

Elaine gets up to leave, says 'Thank you for taking the time to see me, I will be in touch within a week with the breakdown and treatment.'

Back at the office the very first thing to do is write all of this up, enclose the notes and scribbles from the meeting, and put it in the production diary.

This is the initial meeting with a client. What would you have done or said differently? Do you rate Elaine's communication skills as highly as your own? Have you learnt any little tricks that will be helpful to you?

'Paperwork' is generally regarded as boring. By being involved with the process of getting and then producing video programmes you will find it more interesting. The paperwork saves you getting brain overload by trying to remember too much. It also tells the story of your success from start to finish. Paperwork has a purpose: when you need information or facts in the future it will be there in your production diary. The production diary should ensure that anyone can recreate your programme exactly.

Now Elaine and Simon will sit down and discuss the meeting and work out some figures and a treatment. You will remember that Simon guessed at around £10,000. Now they have enough information to be much more accurate. The agreement is that these initial stages are not charged. That is the way most companies work. The cost can usually be hidden somewhere in the overall budget. You could have discussed 'Cost of development work' at the meeting, but I leave it to you to decide the morals and ethics of charging someone to give you a job!

Budgets – overview

Before we look at what goes into a budget we need to consider what a budget really is. The idea of a budget is to approximate as closely as possible how much every detail of a programme will cost. We allow a sum of money to each part of the programme, whether it is a performer, a location shoot or lunch for the crew.

It is essential that these figures are as accurate as possible so that we can see, during the production, if we are going 'over budget' (spending too much), or 'under budget' (not spending what was allocated). We need these figures so that we don't go to the client after we have made the programme and ask for twice as much as we originally quoted. He probably won't pay and we will be the losers.

Not everything can be costed accurately; only with experience can we get better. We can build in 'contingency' to cover odd little mistakes, but the danger of that lies in over estimating and costing the programme too high for the client to agree to. We lose the programme unnecessarily.

In reality there are three budgets we need to complete. One is the 'client budget', one the 'predicted budget' and the last is the 'actual budget'.

The client budget is a summary sheet of the predicted budget. Remember the client wants to know what the programme will cost. It is fair and reasonable for him to see how you arrived at a final figure, but he really won't be interested in how many sandwiches were eaten or how much sugar went into the tea. Neither is it a good idea for him to know how much profit you made.

The predicted budget is an estimate of exactly what money is allocated to what item in the production process. The whole process from letters and stamps to hiring crew and doing the post production must be estimated as closely as possible. There are lots of suggested headings, as you would imagine, and these will be dealt with later under 'budgets'.

The actual budget is the real cost of all the items that make up the programme. Using the same headings as before the actual cost is noted down. This enables us to check whether our estimate was accurate or not. Comparing these two figures will allow us to see whether we are over or under budget as the programme progresses. This way we can make corrections as we go along, avoiding any possible nasty shocks at the end, which could result in us having an embarrassing meeting with the client.

There are no rules to laying out your budget, but I would suggest it is helpful to have the items in one column, the predicted figures in the next column followed by the actual figures. You will see a budget sheet later in the book.

I suggest that for the client budget it is easier for the client to understand if you break down the whole programme into the three areas of pre production, production and post production. Often you will see a further area called indirect costs; these are costs for lawyers, accountants and contingency. There are no rules and you may want to break it down further. Certainly you will need an idea of all the figures in case the client says 'how much is the studio costing us?' or 'why is pre production so high?'

The 'proper' budget, the one I am calling the 'predicted' budget will take a long time to draw up because everything connected with the programme must go into it. Unless you are given the Fashions for You programme there is no point in wasting time trying to construct a budget before you have the programme and have agreed a format. This leaves us with a big dilemma, how do we construct the client budget without wasting a lot of time?

Some people will tell you of 'magic formulae', some will say 'guess', and some will say 'use your experience'. It may be possible to be reasonably accurate with a magic formula and this is certainly a starting point. A short corporate video of this type, with very little enhancement (famous artists, known pop songs, complicated effects, etc.) often does work out at about £1500 a running screen minute. A five minute programme costing about £7500 would have pre production of about £2500, production of about £3000 and post production of about £2000.

The more programmes you do, the better you will get at estimating the cost. Until then let's see if we can find some pointers to a quick estimate.

The pre production stage contains all the meetings, phone calls, letters, research, location visits, scripts, storyboard and so on. Who is going to do all that? If it is you, how much will you charge? Are you worth £5 per hour or £25? How long will it take you? A day, a week or a month? The more planning, the less time in studio or on location. Pre production is cheaper than production.

For the production stage you will get quite accurate ideas by spending a few minutes looking at rate cards from production and hire companies. How much does a crew cost for the day? When the Fashions for You programme was discussed at the meeting, it was suggested that the local fashion college might provide models. It would be sensible to ring up and find out (a) will they supply them, and (b) how much for? Elaine also said that a friend might compose some music for the programme. Again, ring up and ask will he and how much. How long will it take to shoot this programme? A day in studio and a day on location? A week in studio and a month on location?

Post production is the editing, audio dubbing, effects and general tidying of the programme. How much is an edit suite for a day with an operator? How much is audio post production? How long will it take?

Fortunately you are not working completely blind. Your course will have taken you through a series of exercises already. You have probably done scripts, shooting and editing for months. You know roughly how long it takes. Most companies will work on a day shooting equals a day editing for location work. You may already have found this is a bit optimistic. Or maybe you have found that spending longer on the planning you can cut this down to a day shoot and half a day edit. Maybe you have had such a lovely time shooting anything that moves without planning anything and then found yourself in edit for a month!

We will come back to the budget later. For now we are only going to estimate the three areas so we have something for Mr Hermandes within a week. We will give him a breakdown of a five to six minute programme costing £2800 for pre production, £3750 for production and £2750 for post production, leaving £700 for the indirect costs. This is a total delivered cost of £10,000. It may look like a contrived, convenient figure (which it is!), but it is a starting point. We can tell him that we are looking at a fair estimate. It is unlikely to be more and will probably be less. We need the programme content agreed before we can get any more accurate.

Phone calls and letters

When we looked at 'requests for a programme' we started to discuss the basic communication skills used in phone calls and letters. Simon now needs to find out if his friend would be interested in composing some music, and if the college would be interested in providing models.

There are no rules or a 'right way' to make phone calls or write letters. There are, however some important points to bear in mind. In this case this is a business conducting itself in a professional manner. It might be a friend that Simon has to ring but this is not a social chat, it is a business proposition. Phones cost money and time costs money. We need to say what we have to say as concisely as possible, in as short a time as possible, while remaining professional and, at the same time, listening to and understanding what is being said to us.

It is sensible to jot down what you want to say, not word for word but the main points. That way you don't forget anything and have the embarrassment of ringing back. Simon gets his notebook, looks up Julian's phone number and puts at the top of the page *'Fashions for You – possible soundtrack – Phoned Julian (6874 476201) 21st July.'* This identifies this sheet of paper as yet another that is going into the production diary.

Fashions for You - possible Soundtrack - Phoned Julian (6874 476201) 21st July. Possibly doing a video on Fashion. Interested in doing the music? Punchy, about 5 minutes, how much? When? Chance of a bar or two for a meeting? Put it in writing!

Simon rings Julian and, remembering this is a professional call not a social 'mates down the pub' call, identifies himself as 'Julian, this is Simon from Ace Productions'. You can see from the note what Simon wants. He will be honest and say 'we haven't got the programme yet', he will tell Julian the style of music and its approximate length. He wants to know how much it will cost (roughly) and how long it will take. The note 'chance of a bar or two for a meeting?' is something Elaine and Simon like to do, and you might copy. When they send the costing and treatment to the client they also send a cassette with some sample music on it. There are two reasons for this. The first is that when I say to you the music will be punchy and vibrant, you have a sound going round in your head, which is punchy and vibrant. It probably is nothing like the one that is in mine! So that there is no misunderstanding, Simon and Elaine make up a short cassette of a couple of library music tracks (and in this case, Julian's) so that the client can hear the sort of music they are thinking of.

The second reason is more subtle. It shows the client that they have already started to develop the programme. This makes it a bit more difficult for the client to turn them down. It is possible that the client may like the music enough to want it, and therefore pay a little more than he originally said he had in his budget. I don't guarantee it, but anything you can do to make the client feel special can only help your cause.

The last note is important. This is a professional call; Julian won't have all the answers immediately. If he rings back with the answers there is only hearsay evidence of what was said. If you ask him to write to you with the answers, the figures and dates could form part of a contract. There is evidence of what he said, and, of course, something else to go in the production diary!

Now for the college. This is a different phone call. They are not like your friend. Simon does not even know the name or title of the person he wants to speak to. The switchboard operator won't help. He needs to sell the idea as being of benefit to the college. Why don't you write some notes and then compare them with Simon's. Two heads are better than one and both of you may have some ideas the other could use.

> *Fashions for You - Models - Phoned Genie College (923871) 21/7*
>
> *Head of Drama Dept.? Identify. Possible prog coming up. Interested in some of*
>
> *the girls getting TV experience? Credits.*
>
> *Need 3 or 4 in about three weeks. Cost? Backup letter. Name, Address*

Simon is going to call the college and ask to speak to the head of the drama department. If he just asks for the drama department, he will probably get a staff room or a secretary. Neither of these is wrong, it is just that they will probably have to refer him to someone else, wasting time and money.

The 'identify' note is to remind him to start by saying this is Simon, the production manager from Ace Video Productions.

As with Julian, there are no promises here, he is enquiring whether they would be interested in a possible programme.

The 'experience in TV' comment is to remind him that there must be some benefit for the college. Equally the 'credits' comment. He will say 'of course we will credit the college with supplying the models'.

If all this seems a possibility then he can go on to say that he will need them for probably a day in three or four weeks time. He needs to know how much will be charged. The college may have an idea or it may be that Simon pays the girls direct.

Whatever the result of this telephone conversation is he will send a 'back up letter', confirming what has been said. Even if it is a negative response from the college, it does no harm to say thank you for your time.

The final 'name, address,' is very important. Do not forget to get the name of the person you spoke to. You cannot address a letter 'to the person I spoke to on the telephone today'! It is possible that Simon spoke to the deputy head or a head of section. The telephone operator put him through to someone, but not necessarily the head. The address should be a confirmation; Simon has already got the address from the phone book when he looked up the number.

I am not going to spend time on telling you everything that was said, I am sure you know how to conduct telephone conversations, suffice it to say that the head of department agreed in principle but needs to speak to a couple of people about the details. He introduced himself as Joe Martin and would have to speak to the head of production, Sally Beagle, before clearing it with the principal.

Simon adds notes to his original note with details of the conversation and, yes you guessed, files it in the production diary.

At this stage there is only one letter that Simon needs to write. Like business telephone calls, business letter writing is a basic communication skill, which I am sure you have been taught. The basics are to keep it short and to the point. Include any and every thing that is relevant. Make sure there are no ambiguities. It should be clear what the letter is about and what you want the recipient to do about it. Is this a 'for information' letter, a 'please reply to these points' letter. Are you asking for information? Do you need a reply by a certain date? Do you need a reply in writing?

Simon will write to the college, on company paper, thanking them for their interest and confirming what has been said so far. He will suggest that he needs a provisional agreement as soon as possible, and will let them know as soon as there is a new development.

It may be that if you are finding this simulation helpful, you would like to construct your own letter now, bearing in mind the above points.

You will find Simon's letter on the next page and can compare it with your own. Once again, there are no rights or wrongs, just a few do's and don'ts, so your letter is probably just as good, if not better. Check that it has all the points that need covering included.

If you compare this letter with yours, you will see that Simon has tried to be formal but friendly; he has made it clear that he needs an agreement in principle as soon as possible and has covered the detail of cost, credits, transport and meals.

You will notice that this letter contains three important ingredients, which I will call *what, why* and *when*. There is no room left in the letter for any misunderstanding or need to waste precious time, by the college asking questions, if these three ingredients are included. The college has been told what is required, why it is required and when it is required (four or five models for a studio catwalk shoot within three to four weeks).

Does your letter contain 'what, why and when'? If not do you understand the sense of including them?

We could simply have written saying 'I asked this morning if you could supply four or five girls for a studio catwalk shoot in three or four weeks. Please let me know if this can be arranged'. Not very friendly, quite formal but OK. Assume you are the head of department, which letter is most likely to prompt you into finding a way of supplying these girls? You would probably rather have the one that says 'thank you for your time' and 'I realize you will have to consult with people', than the two lines saying 'Can I have the girls'?

You will have to write a lot more letters before we finish this programme. It will help you to remember that they will all follow the same format. Be polite. Say thank you. Include what, why and when.

No two letters from different people can be identical. Each person will put what he or she wants to say in his or her own words. What I am suggesting is that all the letters anyone writes in connection with a video programme should have the same content. It goes without saying that the letters will be word processed. The days of trying to decipher someone's hand written scrawl are long gone. Perhaps your mother would like to see your handwriting, because it makes it more personal! Business letters are business letters and word processors these days do all the hard work for you. They can spell check, grammar check and allow you to try out different formats and styles without losing the content.

I will let you into a little secret about Ace Productions. All the hand written notes, plans and diagrams concerned with their programmes are scanned into the computer. These together with the word processed material are carefully indexed so that the whole production diary is also on disk. If there is a need for Simon or Elaine to reference something quickly it is easily retrieved.

You may think this is a good enough idea to 'borrow' for your production diary, but remember there must be original hard copy, as well, in case something goes wrong and you need to produce the original document.

Ace Productions
Video Programmes on Budget & on Time

39, West Street
Genie Town
GT64 6DE

Tel: 96795 230871
Fax: 96795 230858

Mr. Joe Martin
Head of Drama   21st July 1999
Genie College
Little Road
Genie Town GT16 4DX

Dear Mr Martin,

Thank you for spending the time talking to me on the telephone this morning, and your interest in our possible need for models for a video. We should know within a week or two whether we are commissioned to make the programme.

If we are to make the video, time will be tight which is why I suggested to you that we would need four or five girls in three or four weeks time. There is to be one 'catwalk' sequence and we anticipate that it will take a day in studio.

I am sure the girls will find the experience of working in the video, rather than the stage, medium interesting and exciting. Of course they will have their names in the credits and, I am sure, we can provide them with a tape of their performance.

It will be helpful if you could give me an indication of cost, and available days, in order for me to complete my scheduling. We will, of course, provide transport and meals.

I fully understand that you will need to speak to Sally Beagle and the Principal before you can commit yourself, but I would be grateful if you could write and let me know if we have a provisional agreement at your earliest convenience.

I will contact you as soon as we have any new information.

Once again thank you for your interest.

Yours sincerely,

Simon Kent

Simon Kent.   Production Manager

The treatment

While Simon is dealing with Julian and the college, Elaine decides to give some thought to the treatment of this programme. The only thing to do is sit down with a cup of coffee and think through the programme.

Elaine has now got the basic idea of the programme; she knows the area we are working in. We called this the aim. 'We will do something to promote this range of exciting, affordable quality clothing'.

She knows precisely which aspect we will deal with. The objective. 'We will do a short (5–7 minute) promotional programme, promoting the "Fashions for You" range of clothing to buyers visiting their trade stand. The video will stop passing trade which will assist the sales staff in increasing their output to retail stores'.

She knows who we are expecting to watch the programme. The target audience. 'Retail buyers at a trade fair'.

What Elaine doesn't know is how she is going to do it.

The treatment of a programme is the beginning of its creation. The treatment will state how the programme will take shape. All the ideas we had when we were thinking about the programme can now be brought together into a simple document, which follows the programme from opening to end. The treatment is a very important stage in the production process. When a client is involved and we have been asked to make a programme for that client, the aim, objective and target audience will have been supplied, or, as in this case, it has been deduced from the original request.

Elaine has been asked to go away and come up with a treatment. This gives the client a basic working document that shows precisely how we are going to do his or her programme. It is neither a script (but the script will come from the treatment), nor a visualization (but the pictures and sound will also come from the treatment).

To help in the construction of a treatment it is necessary to have lots of ideas about the programme written down, ideas about the type of music, ideas about the type of shots, ideas about the type of words to be spoken, ideas about the type of performers, ideas about the types of locations and so on.

The treatment will pull all of these together in a logical order so that the client can get the overall feel of the programme. This makes it a lot easier to discuss precise areas of script or precise locations that will be part of the programme.

The problem with this treatment is that the Fashions for You programme does not technically have a beginning or end. Because people will not sit down and watch it, but walk past it at any moment in its showing, Elaine suggested, at the client meeting, that the programme would be a series of cameos, showing the process of design, manufacture and the range of clothing. She sips her coffee and thinks. She is imagining she is at the trade fair and passes the Fashions for You stand. She sees a designer working on rough layouts of a casual shirt. Now what? She imagines she is busy, has lots of stands to look at and walks on. She has not seen the finished shirt or its manufacture. How then can we show all three stages at once?

Elaine has realized how easy it would be to make a programme that failed completely because it spent three minutes on design, followed by three minutes on manufacture, ending with three minutes of the actual clothes.

Constructing a treatment is, arguably, the most creative part of the whole process of production. The whole programme has to be described, on paper, so that the client can 'see and feel' it for himself. Perhaps you would like to help Elaine by jotting down a few notes on how she could show all three processes in a coordinated, but short, space of time.

How are we going to do this programme? What sort of visuals will we use? What sorts of sounds are there? What sorts of performers are involved? Do we use a voice track? How are we going to start?

The treatment also gives a starting point for the dialogue that will follow when we sit down with the client and discuss the programme. Often a client will have ideas for the programme that, perhaps, haven't yet quite formed. The problem we are faced with is how do we get the ideas out of the client's head and into our treatment. It may be that the client will like the opening but, for example, want the order reversed. Start with the factory and then go to the designers. There should be enough flexibility in the treatment to have things moved around, or added to. Nothing is yet fixed. The ideas have been put on paper and communicated. The treatment shows how we are going to 'treat' the programme. What is important is that the whole thing is described in sounds and pictures to build up an idea of how we are going to make this programme.

Elaine is going to put the ideas she has on paper, in any order, as they come to her and then show them to Simon to try and form a cohesive outline.

Punchy, vibrant music with pictures cutting on the beat. Use logo (with special effects) to link. Close ups of manufacture. 'Real' designers working in mid shot. Mix designs to catwalk. Mix close ups of factory with close up of catwalk. Use split screens and quarter screens to include logo and processes of manufacture. Superimpose model credits over catwalk long shots. Use coloured moving lights on catwalk shots. Limited use of voice over to cover the cuts.

Elaine asks Simon if he has got a few minutes to run through her ideas. In a more formal sense this meeting could be called a production meeting. Production meetings are any meetings that involve two or more people that are directly concerned with the production. We will cover them later, but for now we will settle for Elaine and Simon chatting about the treatment.

Elaine explains her thoughts. She can see that the shots will be cut to the beat of the music; this will allow pictures to change quite quickly in a natural way. The shot lengths will, therefore, be short. She sees the Fashions for You logo being used to link shots that would otherwise not cut together naturally. The special effects to be used on the logo will be, typically, to rotate it, streak it, or zoom it out of a visual of the product. She sees the designer shots being mid shots of the designers working on their ideas and layouts. Elaine explains that she can see possible links by using cuts or mixes from a design to the catwalk or from the factory to the catwalk. This would allow for the product, design, manufacture and logo to be shown continuously within about 30 seconds to a minute. There is no beginning or end as such so a credit for the models could be super-imposed over one of the catwalk shots. Ace Productions' credit could lead into a Fashions for You logo, as could a credit for Julian, if they use his music. It may be possible to use split or quarter screens for one sequence, although Elaine realizes that the playback monitor will be very small and they will have to choose the images carefully. A carefully chosen voice track will be used to cover the cuts between the various stages.

PROPOSED TREATMENT FOR FASHIONS FOR YOU VIDEO

The programme begins with a few seconds of punchy, vibrant music that has a strong beat and rhythm over a black screen. This music will run throughout the programme and its beat will allow cutting of different shots to the music. Fashions for You logo fades up from black and is mixed with a long shot of a catwalk parade of the range of clothing. A neutral accent, mature male voice states 'this is the exciting, yet affordable, range of clothing everybody wants today'.

On the beat, we cut to a mid shot of a designer working on a casual shirt; the voice over covers this transition with ' by employing the best designers Fashions for You are in touch with the youth of today'.

We mix back to the catwalk, this time in mid shot to show the shirt collection. A Fashions for You logo fades into the picture and the two images then spin into a mid shot of the factory floor. The voice over picks this shot up with ' carefully crafted to exacting standards, these are the clothes that are selling today'.

This pattern forms the basis of the programme. The shots will be (e.g.) zoom in from designer to the pattern she is working on, mix to a factory shot in close up showing the care taken with production, cut to close up of girl on catwalk, zoom out to mix with Fashions for You logo, cut to another design. The programme will use short length shots both in close up and medium long shot of the three stages from design through manufacture to catwalk parade. In order to avoid a predictable repetition the shot lengths and order of transitions will change with the programme.

The Fashions for You logo will appear both on its own and mixing with moving shots two or three times a minute. This logo will be animated in transition to avoid static and repetitious shots.

The voice over will be kept to a minimum and be restricted to linking images with short phrases such as 'look at the care that goes into crafting this range of affordable designs'.

The programme will have a total running time of five to six minutes when it will naturally cut back to the beginning. There will be two subtly displayed credits, one for the models and one for Ace Productions.

Simon agrees that he can see the general concept but points out that they must produce a programme that, technically, has a beginning and an end. Of course the end must link into the beginning, because it will be shown continuously, but that is their problem. He feels that Mr Hermandes is looking for a treatment that describes how they will deal with the programme from beginning to end and not as something that has no beginning or end.

They talk it through for about an hour and then Elaine sits down with the word processor and does a first draft of the treatment.

Elaine prints a couple of copies and goes back to Simon for another production meeting. They know that a treatment is supposed to describe how they see the programme developing. It is the first attempt at creation. It is natural to leave it as fluid as possible. Expressions such as 'the voice-over will use these type of words', 'the pictures will show this sort of image' are common in treatments. The idea at this stage is that you have a creative idea of how the programme will look and feel that you can convey to the client. Nothing is cast in stone; the treatment will be the central discussion point if the client wants you to go ahead with production. It is the storyboard that maps out the entire programme shot by shot and, because this is an expensive and time consuming process, it is implicit that fees have to be agreed before we spend any more 'free time' on developing the programme.

While Elaine has been working on the treatment, Simon has been busy listening to music tracks from the library music CDs, and has copied a few of them onto cassette. They look at the treatment and listen to the tracks. Already we have the opening feel of the programme, we can 'see' the images and imagine the complimentary sounds. The precise locations are not necessary, what is needed is an overall view of how the programme runs. They both agree that there is enough 'feel' in the treatment to send it to Mr Hermandes and they listen to Simon's selection of music.

Although the music tracks are different, the same theme of youthful, bright, punchy beat is obvious in all of them. Two of them have both Elaine and Simon tapping out the beat on the table. It is these two that are the obvious choices to send to Mr Hermandes. There is no word from Julian and his music track yet, and they decide to give him another day to come up with something.

While Simon works out a breakdown of the budget that was asked for you might like to compare your treatment with this one. You will see that neither can be the same. Equally one is not better than the other. Your programme and Ace Productions will both work. The dilemma is that Mr Hermandes may well have asked three producers for treatments and cost. The programme that is commissioned is the one that Mr Hermandes likes the feel of most. Is there anything in Elaine's treatment that you might want to borrow to change yours? Is there anything in yours that Elaine might want to borrow?

Client budget

Simon knows that the client had suggested they had a budget of about £8000. He also knows this is unrealistic for the programme they want to do. Ace Productions do not want to compromise their programme, so what do we do about this shortfall of £2000? You think about it while Simon prepares his budget.

Simon will show this to Elaine and they will sit down to discuss the covering letter that will go with the treatment and client budget. You will see that, although the two of them have different roles, they are working as a team. They have spent a reasonable amount of time on this programme already, even though they may not get it. This is perfectly normal in business. You would get two or three quotes for work you wanted done on your house, for instance, which would involve the suppliers spending time in trying to come up with the work you require at an acceptable price and with an acceptable result. The trick is for you not to tell the supplier exactly how much you are prepared to spend and for the supplier to come up with something special that you are prepared to buy.

What Simon has done is to give rounded figures, in the three areas, which are moveable downwards. Everybody is then happy, the client will have 'knocked some off the bill' and you will have got the price you wanted.

Elaine gets her notepad out and the two then decide on the content of the letter that will, hopefully, persuade Fashions for You to commission them to do the video.

PROVISIONAL BUDGET FOR FASHIONS FOR YOUR VIDEO

This provisional budget is based on the programme outlined in the enclosed treatment. It has to make assumptions based on experience and should be used as a guide only.

The figures are broken down into the three stages the programme will go through and are maximum costs in each area. Unless major changes are made to the programme structure, as outlined in the treatment, these figures will not be exceeded.

Savings can be made, which may compromise the quality and effectiveness of the programme. These are outlined at the end.

Pre Production (research, location visits, scripts, storyboard, contracts, clearances, general admin.)		£2800 : 00
Production (crew, production staff, performers, video, lighting and sound)		£3750 : 00
Post Production (editing, audio dubbing, effects)		£2750 : 00
Indirect Costs (Legal, Financial)		£ 700 : 00
	TOTAL	**£10,000 : 00**

Savings can only realistically be made in the production and post production stages.

As this is to be a continuous programme we could have less variety of shots and a shorter length overall. This would cut crew costs and time of shooting.

We could cut the studio catwalk scenes and replace them with location shots at one of the two locations (design office or factory). This would cut the studio booking and crew costs, but would add an amount to the location costs.

We could cut the voice-over, saving the artist costs and a percentage of audio dubbing.

We could cut the special effects used to link the logo and the picture track, cutting the post production costs.

A combination of these cuts would bring the programme nearer to the £8000 suggested, but would obviously compromise the quality and excitement of the finished product.

Thanks. Enclosed, treatment and Cost.

Explain music cassette.

Opportunity to discuss further.

Models.   Julian's music.

Meeting?

Before they can write to Mr Hermandes, Julian rings to say that he has come up with some examples of the sort of music he could produce. He will put the cassette in the post with an idea of costs and the time he will need to complete it if they want to go ahead.

Because we have already spent some time on letters, I will leave it to you to write the letter to Mr Hermandes, or imagine what is in it. You can guess the content from Elaine's note. There will, of course, be reference to 'the music we can have specially commissioned for you' and 'meeting?' on the note will be translated into 'We would be pleased to have a further meeting to discuss any of the detail or costing of the programme.'

Elaine will send the letter and cassette Recorded Delivery to ensure that it can be tracked and she will know it has arrived. Some companies use a courier service; some will have a junior assistant who will deliver it. The point is not 'how it is delivered' but 'have you got a signature for it', and a record of it arriving. If you know it arrived, and you haven't heard anything within a reasonable space of time, it is fair to assume the letter you will get will be a 'thank you, but no' letter!

Negotiations and costs

A few days have gone by and a letter arrives from Joe Martin regarding the girls needed for the catwalk sequence.

Simon and Elaine are very pleased with this. Even if they don't get the Fashions for You programme, they have established a very important link together with the offer of the use of Genie College's facilities. This may be very useful in future productions.

Genie College
Little Road

Genie Town GT16 4DX

Joe Martin	Telephone: 96795 230871 Ext. 321
Head of Drama Department	Fax: 96795 230858

26th July 1999

Simon Kent
Production Manager
Ace Productions
39, West Street
Genie Town GT64 6DE

Dear Mr Kent,

The Principal, Sally Beagle and I have discussed your possible need for some of our girls to act as models in a video.

We feel that while this would be a good experience for them, college work must come first and they could not be spared on a course day. Sally has spoken to the final year group about this project and several would be prepared to give up an evening or two.

The Principal raised an interesting point by asking if it would be possible to mock up a catwalk in our theatre for the filming. He feels the experience could then be extended to others in the course.

Regarding cost, we would prefer to discuss that if this project becomes a reality. The feeling is that there would be a charge for our facilities and a small fee for the girls, which could be paid directly to them, to recompense them for giving up their evening.

I realize that everything is very fluid at the moment, but if this seems a possibility, and you are going ahead with the video, perhaps we could speak then.

Yours Sincerely

JOE MARTIN

Joe Martin. Head of Dept.

Simon will write back thanking Mr Martin for his prompt and positive response. He will say that it may be possible to make use of their facilities and he doesn't see a problem with evenings. He cannot say 'we will use your facilities' because Fashions for You may want 'real' models and a studio. He cannot promise anything because Ace Productions have not yet got a programme to produce.

You will find your programmes will run more smoothly if you are honest and do not promise things that you cannot deliver. To write back and say 'yes, we will use your theatre and want six girls in two weeks' would be very difficult to cancel, if you don't get the programme, and would wreck your chances of ever using that contact again!

I know of some enthusiastic students who told passers by in the street that they were from the BBC, doing an item for the evening news. They ended up in the Police Station and the college had to apologize to the BBC!

The next day another letter arrives. This one is for Elaine. It has a Fashions for You logo on the envelope. Elaine and Simon know this is crunch time. They make a cup of coffee and open it.

This is an interesting letter, and typical. Elaine has done enough at the initial meeting to impress Mr Hermandes with her professional approach. Simon and Elaine have gone to an amount of trouble with simple early research to produce a treatment that the client likes. The client knows that a proper budget cannot be worked out without accurate details of exactly what is required, but accepts that the programme's estimated cost is about right.

It is possible that another producer has got a similar letter, so what happens next is very important. This is where Elaine's negotiating skills are required. She will arrange another meeting, but first Simon must look at specific areas of his budget. He now needs to negotiate with the intended suppliers and try to get more accurate figures.

As you will have realized, all of this initial procedure is taking time, for which no money has changed hands. The delicate balance of negotiation lies in its two definitions, one is to come to an agreement about (the programme cost), the other is to overcome an obstacle (the client wants the programme, but does not have the money). Somehow we have to agree a fair cost and end up making the programme.

You cannot suddenly drop a couple of thousand pounds off the price of the same programme. Either the programme has to change or you have to accept a lower profit margin. In reality the result will probably be a

FASHIONS FOR YOU
exciting, affordable clothing for you

21, Gothic Road
Genie Town
GT64 2TX

Telephone: 96795 376281   *Fax: 96795 397401*

Ace Productions
39 West Street
Genie Town GT64 6DE

2nd August 1999

Dear Elaine Booker,

Thank you for the treatment, costing and music cassette for our intended video.

We have discussed the contents at some length and, whilst we are pleased with the treatment ideas, we are concerned that the cost is higher than we had expected, and higher than our budget.

It is obvious that you have gone to a lot of trouble on our behalf and we particularly liked the catwalk idea and two of the extracts of music.

As you will be aware we have contacted other production companies and have now had a chance to see their ideas and compare them with yours.

We would like the opportunity to explore your ideas further and, particularly, discuss the costing, and suggest we have a further meeting before we make any decisions.

We do realize that time is tight if we are to have a finished product for the next trade fair and, because of this, perhaps you would be good enough to telephone my secretary to make an appointment.

Yours sincerely,

Pat Hermandes

Pat Hermandes

Projects Officer

combination of both. If you go back to Simon's original budget statement, you will see that the only areas that could be cut were the
production and post production stages. The pre production stage is pretty
well fixed because the time spent on research, writing, location visits,
bookings and so on will not be massively affected by small cuts and alter-
ations to the programme.

A major influencing factor with this particular programme, and a
strong negotiating tool, is whether Fashions for You can be persuaded
to pay for a 'tweak' to the programme to make it more suitable for the
other target audience, the customer in the shop, and whether they will
pay for updates to the programme to include seasonal changes.

It may be that the cost of the shop outlet copy, which only involves
different editing, a couple of additional shots and a slightly different
voice-over, would be minimal if shot and edited at the same time and
could be included in the original quoted cost of the trade show
programme. This would provide two programmes for the price of one for
the client and not involve the production company in the greater outlay
of doing the whole thing again at a later date.

There are options that involve the actual payment of money. It is
perhaps not ethical for companies to keep suppliers waiting for payment,
but it is quite usual. This gives everyone a cash flow problem and can
seriously damage a small company. It is possible to negotiate 'prompt
payment terms' so that you get paid in stages, by your client, whilst the
production is being made, which in turn means you can negotiate reduc-
tions for crew, studios, editing suites and so on if you offer them
payment on completion of their service.

Beyond these negotiating tools there is one more. If staged payments
are accepted by the client, it is usual to present an invoice for approximately a third of the cost when the storyboard has been agreed. It may
be that the client will accept a charge for a detailed budget before he
commissions a programme. This means that you get paid something for
all the work you have done so far and the additional work involved in
drawing up an accurate budget. Of course the client has the option of
looking at a detailed budget and still not commissioning the programme.
With large productions clients may pay for a budget and a storyboard
before agreeing to a programme.

Client meeting – negotiations

Elaine has telephoned Mr Hermandes' secretary and arranged a meeting for the following afternoon. These are the notes she will take with her.

Mr Hermandes - 2.30 p.m. 5th August. Negotiations.

Costs based on experience. No research done into locations, performer costs.

Figures quoted are top figures, final amount will probably be lower.

Could negotiate retail outlet programme to be done at same time.

Could negotiate seasonal tweaks.

Prompt, staged payments?

Simplified, rather than graphic, storyboard.

Simon suggested cut the catwalk, voice-over, special effects on logo links.

We cannot spend more time and money and not charge.

Suggest £300 for storyboard and full budget, to be included in cost if programme accepted.

Time is now critical to both parties!

Elaine meets Mr Hermandes as arranged and has with her a folder containing her notes, the treatment, Simon's budget and the letters that have been received and sent so far.

Before we see what happens next why don't you imagine you are Elaine? How are you going to handle this crucial meeting? Agree to anything to get the programme? Refuse to move from the original figures? Agree to make a sub standard programme for the figure you are offered? What are you prepared to negotiate?

Now imagine you are Mr Hermandes. How are you going to get the programme outlined in the treatment at a reduced cost? What are you prepared to compromise over? It often helps at this stage if you practice conducting meetings with a friend. You have enough information about this programme now to try it out. You role-play Elaine while your friend plays Mr Hermandes, swap over roles and do it again. What did you learn from this exercise? Do you now feel more confident about negotiating? Personal presentation and communication skills are key to succeeding in this business. Do you have them?

Mr Hermandes and Elaine have sat down and Mr Hermandes starts by saying *'I will be honest with you, Elaine, we like the programme treatment and the music very much. We have had the chance to see other suggestions and would like to come down in favour of yours, the sticking point is the money. So where do we go from here?'*

Now what? The ball is very firmly in Elaine's court. They want her programme, but they can't afford it. This is not about 'how do we convince him our programme is best', this is about 'how do we agree a figure'.

It is not a good idea to go straight in and say 'how much will you pay'. This is negotiation, not confrontation! Let's see what Elaine comes up with.

'I'm pleased that you like the programme. We spent a lot of time thinking about how to do it in an exciting and effective way. You haven't said which music you like, but I hope it is the piece we can have done specially for you, Julian is very good and we use him for a lot of our programmes.

Simon has highlighted the areas in which we could make savings by cutting the catwalk sequences, the voice-over or the special effects with your logo. I think this would detract from the programme. Maybe we should look at other areas first.

I am sure you will realize that we can only spend so much time on developing a programme before it becomes an untenable cost to us. Can I ask what your top figure is and then we can see how close we can get?'

This is a good start. Elaine has subtlety suggested they could have a unique theme tune, and to tinker too much with the programme will leave them less than satisfied. She has also made it clear that they are not going to be able to waste any more time (and, therefore, their money) on taking this any further without some payment.

We won't follow the whole conversation. If you look back at the notes Elaine made for the meeting you will see what she is hoping for.

The negotiations are resolved by Mr Hermandes saying that they cannot pay a penny more than £8000, which is more than they origi- nally budgeted for, but that figure would only be available for the programme outlined in the treatment. He has agreed to a simplified storyboard. He does want Julian's music. He will discuss the prompt staged payments with the sales department. He has offered £250 for a storyboard and breakdown budget within seven days provided Elaine can assure him that the programme will be completed for the first trade show on October 16th.

For her part Elaine has decided not to mention the retail outlet programme or the seasonal tweaks. She feels that the offer of £8000 top figure is probably all that is on offer and to suggest they pay more for additional work is not wise at this stage. She has accepted the £250 for the storyboard and budget, provided that she is given a firm yes or no within three days of submitting them. Time, she knows, is the enemy and if this drags on much longer they cannot have a realistic time to produce the programme. She has asked if Simon can have a tour of the design studio and factory within the next couple of days so they can start to plan the location shoots. This has been agreed. Mr Hermandes will be their contact and make the arrangements.

Both parties have given (and taken!) some ground. Negotiation is based on both of you getting the best deal. It is not based on either one of you giving in, or becoming confrontational! It is a difficult, but neces- sary, communication skill which your course should give you plenty of time to practise. The secret is to remain professional, listen to what the other person has to say and then decide whether that is acceptable, or whether you are prepared to go part way towards their viewpoint if they will move a little way towards yours.

This meeting will have to be written up very carefully for the produc- tion file because parts of it contain a verbal contract. We will look at contracts in more detail later, but for the moment you should be aware that if two parties agree to something verbally, what was said forms a contract which can be argued in court if one party defaults on the agreement.

At the end of the meeting Elaine says that she would like to check that she has understood the current position and reads her written notes to Mr Hermandes.

Mr Hermandes - 2.30 p.m. 5th August.

1. We agreed £8K top price for original prog with Julian's music & simple S/board.

2. Submit S/board and budget within 7 days with i/v for £250.

3. Agreement within 2-3 days from that.

4. Complete by 16th Oct. if accepted.

5. Mr H to check on prompt staged payments.

6. Simon to contact Mr H to recce studio & factory in next couple of days.

Mr Hermandes agrees with this and Elaine leaves to put this very important bit of paper in the production diary. She will file it under 'Meetings', but cross reference it to 'Contracts'.

You will often find that one piece of information should really be stored in two places in the production diary. There are two ways of doing this, either cross reference it in the index for each section or, perhaps simpler and quicker to find, copy the original and store the copy in the second location.

Production meetings

Video production involves teamwork and a very high degree of organization. Whatever the part in the whole process it should be done only once, and done by the person allocated to do it. To avoid repetition or, much worse, omission, it is necessary to have team meetings to keep everybody informed and decide on a strategy for the next stage.

The meeting must have one person in charge (the chair person), and that person is responsible for the content, which is written down as an agenda. The meeting should last for a specified time. This avoids irrelevant discussion or the meeting developing into a 'friendly chat'. These meetings should be conducted professionally, with a proper agenda, notes taken and then written up for the production diary. Time is money and the agenda will ensure that the meeting only involves the people concerned and covers only the points needed at this time. The people involved should be given an agenda before the meeting so that they can be properly informed and prepared.

Even if you are working in a very small team, as is the case with Elaine and Simon, you must schedule a meeting for a specific time, with an agenda, and it must last for the minimum time needed to complete that agenda. Production meetings are not about friendly chats, they are about details concerning who does what and by when.

Enthusiasm may well tempt you into popping down to the pub for a meeting. Let me assure you that it will not work, it creates the wrong atmosphere, notes are forgotten about or, at best, are sketchy and you will be deflected from the issue at hand by trying to decide whose round it is next, and by what is going on around you!

Elaine is going to schedule a meeting with Simon for 10 a.m. the next morning. She checks that he will be free and then draws up her agenda.

Fashions for You

Production Meeting   10 a.m. 6th August 1999   Elaine & Simon

AGENDA

1. Review Meeting with Mr Hermandes 5/8/99 (notes attached).
2. Visit to Studio and Factory.
3. Contact Julian.
4. Contact College.
5. Storyboard.
6. Budget.
7. Invoice.
8. Schedule.
9. A. O. B.
10. Date/Time of next meeting.

This meeting should take no longer than 40 minutes.

You will see that item 9 is 'AOB'. This is shorthand for any other business. It is always the item on an agenda after the main body of the meeting has been dealt with. It is designed to allow for any points that may have come up to be covered more fully, or anything that might have been forgotten to be raised. The chair person is responsible for making sure that the matter is pertinent and relevant to this meeting, and may decide to incorporate one, or more, of the points arising as a separate item in the next meeting.

If it is appropriate you may see 'Date/time of next meeting' as the final item on the agenda. This will ensure that everybody present can agree dates and times now, which avoids the time wasting of checking everybody's diary at a later stage.

Notice, also, that Elaine has allowed 40 minutes for this meeting. It isn't always necessary to state a time, but it does help to focus the mind on the business in hand if someone is watching the clock!

This is a formal meeting and Elaine and Simon cannot be disturbed. Elaine has put a message on the answer machine which says 'Thank you for calling Ace Productions. We are sorry that we cannot take your call until 11 a.m. Please leave a message or call back later.' This is polite and honest, the two ingredients of good company communications.

What is discussed at this meeting must go into the production diary, so Elaine will take notes which will be filed with the agenda.

You will notice that Item 1 (review of meeting with Mr Hermandes) has a bracketed 'notes attached'. This means that when Simon received his copy of the agenda he also got Elaine's notes from that meeting. This saves time and allows Simon to be up to speed before the meeting.

Elaine explains why she had no choice but to agree a top price of £8000, which includes Julian's music but a simplified storyboard. Simon agrees that there is probably enough movement in the 'guessed' figures to bring the final figure down. He is not happy that it has to come down that far.

Elaine steers Simon away from a long discussion by pointing out that Items 3, 4, 5 and 6 cover most of what he wants to discuss now! This is the role of the chair person. If the agenda has been drawn up properly, time can be saved by directing the participants of the meeting to cover the item under discussion and not go off at a tangent, wasting time.

If the agenda had only one item ' Discuss what has happened so far', for example, there would be no control or order to the meeting and it would be difficult to make relevant notes.

They move to Item 2. Simon agrees that he will contact Mr Hermandes after the meeting to arrange visits to the studio and factory. Elaine is fairly confident that they will get the programme if Simon can reduce the budget, so they decide that to save time Simon will use the opportunity to do a proper recce of both these locations. This will take longer, but will save time later.

Items 3 and 4 are discussed and Simon agrees to do these as soon as possible. He knows that Julian is not the most reliable composer in the world. He will inform him of the progress so far and ask if he is certain he can deliver the music within a couple of weeks. He will not commission him to write it for a few days, the programme has not yet been given to Ace Productions, and they don't want to pay for something they may not want.

Similarly with the college. Simon will telephone Mr Martin and explain the situation. He wants to explore the possibility of using their theatre, and the cost. This might cut out an expensive studio shoot. Ideally he needs to go and have a look at the facilities.

Elaine agrees to do the storyboard.

Simon will draw up a proper budget, together with the invoice for £250.

Elaine, being the chair person, suggests that they hold over Item 8 (Schedule) until a later meeting, when they know whether or not they have got the programme. This is perfectly normal in meetings. There is no point in doing any more than spending a couple of minutes agreeing that the schedule will be tight, but manageable, and agreeing to discuss it at another meeting.

Under AOB Simon suggests they hire in a temp if they get the programme because of the amount of work that will need to be done in a short time. Elaine suggests Simon costs it out and works out if it can be fitted into the budget.

Elaine moves quickly to Item 10, by saying 'are you OK for 10 a.m. on the 10th?' Simon looks at his diary. He has pencilled in the factory, designers and college for the 9th and 10th, so suggests the 11th and adds that, as Mr H wants the budget and storyboard by the 12th, 8 a.m. might be a better time. Elaine agrees and they both put it in their diaries.

The meeting is concluded at 10.35 a.m., five minutes ahead of schedule.

The official record of the proceedings of this meeting is known as the minutes of the meeting. They will have to go into the production diary, along with the agenda. Elaine uses her notes to type up the minutes, while Simon goes off to make his phone calls.

Fashions for You

Production Meeting   10 a.m. 6th August 1999   Elaine & Simon

MINUTES

1. Agreed top figure of £8000. Simon will find £2000 shortfall by trimming budget.
2. Simon contacting Mr H this afternoon to arrange. He will also conduct a full recce of both sites during his visit.
3. Simon contacting Julian to put him on standby for the music. There is a need to ensure his reliability over deadlines. Price to be discussed.
4. Simon will contact Joe Martin. He hopes to arrange a visit to view the facilities and check whether they would be suitable for the catwalk sequence. Will discuss price.
5. Elaine will do simple storyboard. To be complete within 3-4 days.
6. Simon will work out an accurate predicted budget within 3-4 days and condense down to a client budget for Mr H.
7. Simon will type up an invoice (£250) to Mr H to go with storyboard and budget.
8. Item held over until confirmation that programme has been commissioned.
9. Simon suggests the need for a temp. Will cost it out and check if budget can stand it.
10. Next meeting set for 8 a.m. 11th August 99.

Meeting concluded at 10.35 a.m.

A business caveat

Quite a lot has happened in a short space of time. Let's review what we have got so far.

Ace Productions got a request for a programme by letter. Nothing much happened for about two weeks. This is quite normal, but where does the money come from while you are sitting around in the office? Things then started to happen quite quickly. There is only a week to prepare an accurate budget and do a storyboard. This seven day period involves a weekend. Do you mind working weekends?

Before the budget can be done there are people to contact and arrangements have to be made to do a recce at two locations. There is also the problem of delivery in two months. No crew or performers have been booked, neither has the post production. You cannot deliver the programme on the last possible day, the client might want some late changes. Can you work under this pressure? How good are your organizational and time management skills?

This whole project will take nearly four months to complete. If you are a small outfit (as with Ace Productions), does this mean you can only do three programmes a year? Can you make enough money out of three programmes to support two people and an office? What do you do if you can't?

Part of deciding if you want to start your own company comes from thinking about these questions. Are you happy earning £3000 to £5000 a year and telling your friends you own a video company? What are you going to do if you want more money? Are you prepared to take a part time job, or work evenings at a fast food restaurant? This is the reality of just starting up in business.

Apart from the video production skills do you have business and communication skills? As I asked right at the beginning, are you thinking of making this a part time hobby or a job?

How do Elaine and Simon make money?

Elaine and Simon work mainly in the corporate sector producing short videos for small to medium sized companies. They have built up a nucleus of companies that are constantly wanting their sales and promotional programmes updated. They have all the completed production diaries and, because they know the companies, and the locations, they can do these updates in about a week. This brings in a steady stream of small, but lucrative, work.

Elaine has built up a reputation for her scripts and storyboards, Simon is known for the accuracy of his location recces and production management skills. Quite often one or other of them is called in by another company to do freelance work. Elaine often works as a waitress in the evenings and Simon drives a taxi part time. Both are earning money, not a fortune but enough. The thing that they will both tell you is that they thrive on the hard, pressured work and the creativity they put into it. They haven't found the creation of all the production diaries fun, or exciting, but they compile them meticulously and it pays off when they do repeat business. They have chosen this work. They both agree that they could not work 9 to 5, five days a week!

If you are on a general introductory level course you will be given the opportunity to try all the roles that go into a production. You will learn communication skills, computer skills, organization and management as well as camera, sound and lighting.

You may choose to concentrate on camera operating, or sound recording. Whatever you finally decide you will have a good grounding in all the areas. This is a team game business. Are you improving your team skills?

Elaine and Simon are different, they decided to set up on their own soon after their course. They found it very hard. Most people will become freelance in one area and then gradually get to meet other freelancers in different areas. They may then all get together and form a small company whilst still doing their own freelance work.

Learning is one thing, doing is another. Doing it for lots of money is a quite different ball game!

Let's go back and see what is happening at Ace Productions.

Production planning

Life is about to get very busy. We need a plan to work to. There are lots of ways of looking at production planning and different people will tell you different things. Production planning is not the same as scheduling. It is the planning of the stages of the production, whether it be when to make phone calls, when to book crew or when to go on a location recce. Although both need your time management skills, the simple way of understanding the difference between production planning and scheduling is to think that the production is planned during the pre production stage and then a schedule is drawn up for the actual shooting and post production.

The importance of planning and scheduling is to make sure that you maximize your time by doing things at the right time and in the right order.

Ace Productions build their plan in small bursts when they have lots to do in a short space of time. By writing down the things that need doing nothing gets forgotten. It also helps with their time management. They prioritize things so that they don't do anything twice or have to come back to them because pieces of the jigsaw are missing. Here is Simon's plan.

The first thing that you will notice is, yet again, there is no right or wrong way of doing things. Simon finds it easy to have his plan with him whilst he is doing things, it becomes a sort of notebook. He has a column

			Simon. Production Plan Page 1.
P. L. V. T.	CONTACT	D/T	RESULT
376281	Mr Hermandes		
V. (Factory)	?		
V. (Des)	?		
6874476201	Julian		
230871ε321	Joe Martin		
V. (College)	?		
598406	Bob (Crew)		
T. (Invoice)			
T. (Budget)			

reminding him whether this is a phone call, letter, visit or task (P.L.V.T.). If it is a phone call he writes in the number. If he has the contact name that is written in too, otherwise it has a question mark reminding him to get it. D/T is date or time (or both). If he makes a phone call he writes down the date, this can be referred back to later if it is needed to be included in a letter, for instance. Lastly he has a Results column.

Some people will say it is sufficient to write down what you did and what happened. Some will say you should make a list of what you have to do, and then prioritize it into high, medium or low priority.

My advice is do what works for you. It is your list! You have the time pressure. How is it easiest for you to handle?

More phone calls

Simon decides he will make all the phone calls first. He cannot visit the factory, design studio, or college until he has arranged times and dates, and it is sensible to ring Julian (music) and Bob to put a crew on standby and check the prices.

Starting the budget and doing the invoice depends on when he can arrange his visits.

He makes notes for his phone calls, because he cannot spare the time to keep ringing back if he has forgotten something, and he needs records of the phone calls for the production diary.

Phone Calls - 6/8/99.

1. Mr H - Factory & Studio - When? - Address's? - Contacts? - Bring Video? - Phone Nos. - Parking?

2. Mr M - Visit. - When? - Facilities? - Girls? - Contact? - Parking? - Bring Video? - Cost? - No promises, but looks good.

3. Julian - How much? - Asked once already! - Go for 5 mins with cutting points - Supply on DAT with cassette copy - Confirm next week - must have within a week - Contract.

4. Bob - 2 camera location - Beta - VHS copy BITC - lighting - sound - 2 or 3 days, in a couple of weeks - no promises, but looks good - edit, p. prod ideas?

You will see that planning and preparation is everything. A few minutes spent thinking about what you need to do and ask will save time (and therefore money) in two main ways. You are focused on what you are going to do, increasing your self confidence and putting yourself in the right professional frame of mind, and you can keep the conversation on track and as short as possible. Other people are busy too, they don't want long friendly chats on the phone. They will respond to a professional, well thought out phone call.

We said that everything goes into the production diary. Already we have sections for requests for the programme, letters, phone calls, meetings, contacts, treatment, budgets, and music. Now we are going to open new sections for locations and storyboard.

Already our indexes are becoming complex with cross references. Our heads are beginning to fill up with all the information about the process of production. You can see why it is essential that everything is properly thought out, covered and filed. The result of these phone calls will become part of a contract with the people Simon rings. A verbal contract is very shortly not going to be sufficient. The notes of what Simon wants to say, and the answers he gets back, will be documented.

Imagine how you would feel if you were dealing with someone as unreliable as Julian, if you had done no planning or preparation. You ring up, not really knowing what to say except 'we need some music soon'. You agree to meet for a drink tonight and talk it over. The conversation drifts off to your favourite football teams, and nothing happens until you realize you have no music to play while you are shooting the catwalk scenes. Julian says you didn't give him a date, you say you thought he could work it out, the shoot does not go well, everybody is amazed as what an unprofessional director you are!

Imagine you are Simon. You are going to ring Mr Hermandes. Simon wants to arrange a date and time to visit the factory. He needs the addresses, contact names and phone numbers, and the parking arrangements. He wants to take the office camcorder. Has he left anything out? What would you also need to know? Why does he want to take the camcorder? Why ask Mr Hermandes if he can? Didn't he tell Elaine that he couldn't make a meeting on the 10th because he had pencilled in visits for the 9th and 10th? Did you and Simon forget that the note shouldn't say 'when', but '9th or 10th'? Is there a danger that Mr Hermandes will agree dates and times without asking the other people involved? Should there be a note saying 'ring to confirm the arrangements'?

Now look at the notes for Mr Martin, Julian and Bob (who will arrange his crew). What has been left out? What problems could that throw up? Are you and Simon going to spend the next couple of days on the phone tidying up the loose ends? Is that a good example of time management? Does it look professional?

What have the facilities and the girls got to do with a visit to a head of drama? Why the camcorder, again? What has been left out? Didn't Joe originally suggest evenings only?

Why ask Julian for five minutes with cutting points? Why is there a note that says 'contract' when none of the other phone calls say that?

Why ask Bob for two cameras on location? Isn't location video one camera? What is 'VHS copy BITC' if we are shooting Beta? If Bob supplies crew why ask about edit and post production? Is there anything else you would ask? Would you expect to get all the answers to your questions? What happens if you don't? Should there be a note saying 'send quote'?

Did you think that these are just two or three simple phone calls? Are you beginning to realize the amount of planning and organization that goes with the business you have chosen as a career? Are you beginning to understand why I said at the beginning 'do you just want an expensive hobby'? The business you have decided to enter is mostly planning and preparation with a little bit of shooting, a lot of creativity and endless quantities of 'midnight oil'!

Let's think about some of the questions. Simon wants to take the camcorder because whenever he visits locations he likes to bring back pictures of the location, try out shots to see if the angle or height he wants is possible, hear what the background sound level is and look for dangers that might involve health and safety issues.

If he is planning to use the client's staff in some of the shots it is courtesy to take a couple of minutes to ask if this is OK. That way he can say 'I have permission to take a few sample shots, does anybody object to being in the final video?' You do not want to tie up crew (time and money!) while you try to negotiate with staff.

With the college visit, he is keeping options open that he may use their facilities for the catwalk sequence, instead of a studio. He wants to see if these facilities are suitable and he wants to know how much they will cost. That gives him a comparison for his budget (which has to be done by the 12th!). He wants to see the girls for the same reason as Mr Hermandes' staff. Are they suitable? Do they want to take part? Can he shoot during the day? Evenings will be double time for the crew.

For Julian he remembers his unreliability. You will remember that he did ask last time for, not only a sample cassette, but the approximate cost. He didn't get it. He is going to remind him that, if they get the programme, he will be sent a contract. He wants five minutes, with cutting points, because he doesn't know the precise running time. The cutting points will allow him to extend the five minutes to any length he wants, without noticeable 'jumps' in the music.

Bob will be asked to quote for two cameras on location because this will probably save time, but will cost more. The balance here is whether the time (and money) saved (say a day shooting) outweighs the extra cost. He is working with amateur performers. They will need rehearsing and will not want to do the same things over and over again.

He plans to use one camera for long shots and the other for mid shots and close ups. He has asked for VHS BITC because he will use the office editing suite to do rough cuts. BITC stands for burnt in time code. The actual time code on the original tapes will be displayed within the picture area, helping him to get accurate cutting points.

He needs to ask Bob if he can provide lighting and sound, if not Simon has to arrange it himself. Bob works in the production side of the business. He is the most likely person to know of fairly priced, good editing and post production facilities. Better to say 'Bob recommended you', on the phone, rather than trawl through hours of rate cards.

Let's revise Simon's notes. If you look carefully he has revised the order he wants to say things, to make it more logical. He has also included the telephone numbers. Did you notice they were missing? He will ask Bob if he can come to a meeting. This meeting will be set up before the shoot and they can go through Simon's video of the locations and the storyboard. This means Bob will not be working blind for the shoot nor have any nasty surprises. He will know what shooting, lighting and sound problems there are. Bob may charge Simon to come to this meeting, but it will save time (time is money!) later. Did you think of that? Has Simon left anything out this time? If he rings Mr Hermandes and the phone is engaged, what does he do? If Mr Martin isn't available, or Bob is on a shoot, what now?

Phone Calls - 6/8/99

1. Mr H (376281) - Factory and Studio - ~~When~~ - 9th or 10th? - Addresses - Contacts - Phone Nos. - Parking - ~~Bring video~~ - Explain video, Mr H check if anybody at location objects - Mr H ring when he has made arrangements?

2. Mr M (230871 Ext. 321) - No promises, but looking good. - Visit - ~~When~~ - 9th or 10th? - Address - Contacts - Ext. Nos. - Parking - ~~facilities~~ - -Thinking of using facilities - See them? - Meet girls - ~~Bring video~~ - Explain video - Cost - Get idea of cost before visit . Day shoot?

3. Julian (6874476201) - How much? - Asked once already! - Go for 5 min with cutting points - Supply on DAT with cassette copy - Confirm next week - must have within a week - Contract.

4. Bob (598406) - no promises, but looks good - 2 camera location - Beta - VHS copy BITC - lighting - sound - edit, p. prod ideas? - 2 or 3 days, in a couple of weeks - come to meeting? -

Part of your logical planning will provide the answers, I hope you didn't say 'have a coffee and try later!' We have a busy office to run now. There is a budget to do, as well as the phone calls, and that won't take five minutes.

We have talked about how to conduct yourself during phone calls, so let's précis the result of Simon's.

Mr Hermandes was in a meeting. The secretary asked if she could take a message. Simon viewed this situation as ideal, rather than frustrating, because it gave him the opportunity to ask if Mr Hermandes could make the arrangements for his visits. He asked if Mr Hermandes could ring back confirming which of the two dates would be suitable and what times. He took the opportunity of asking the secretary for the addresses and phone numbers, but didn't mention the video, contact names or if anyone would object to being in the video. Why do you think he left them out? Do you think it was because it is none of the secretary's business or because he wants to keep something secret? Would you have mentioned them anyway?

It is not wrong if you say you would have gone through everything on the list, just different to the way Simon did it. He felt that Mr Hermandes would be the person who knew who to contact, not the secretary, he wanted to discuss bringing the video personally because the reason for it is to do a recce. Ace Productions still have not got this programme, remember. As we have said before, when Elaine enclosed some music samples with the original treatment, it pays to show the client that you are working on the programme even though you haven't got it. Similarly with the employees, it may be that Mr Hermandes has an idea which people he would like to see in the video. Discuss it with him!

The Joe Martin call was similar. He was holding a seminar. Could the secretary take a message. Simon had the production diary in front of him so that he could update it with his notes. He quickly flicked through 'Letters', saw that Joe Martin had to check with Sally Beagle, so asked if she was free. This is a classic use of the production diary being used to save time. Joe Martin would say 'I will have to talk to Sally Beagle about this'. Why not do it the other way round. Explain to Sally and let her discuss it with Joe. She was available, Simon was very careful to say that he couldn't promise anything, but was very hopeful, and thanked her for all their interest and co-operation so far. She thought that Monday evening would be a good time, because she was teaching the group they thought would benefit most in the theatre. This would combine looking at the facilities and talking to the girls. She thought the video could be worked into a course day, she knows that theatre and video are different mediums to work in, and the girls would benefit from the experience. Parking at the theatre building is never a problem. Obviously she has no idea of cost, but she will discuss it all with Joe and he will then ring back. She sounds very enthusiastic and offers Simon her extension number and directions to her office.

Julian, inevitably, isn't answering his phone. Simon is very direct in the message he leaves, starting by saying 'Julian, if you are serious about doing this project, ring me urgently.' He then outlines the running time and the need for cutting points. Simon has dealt with Julian often. The best approach is to be firm, but polite, not show any frustration, but make sure Julian knows exactly what is wanted.

Bob is in and very helpful as usual. He doesn't need to look at his rate card, he knows it by heart. This is a small corporate production and he always makes allowances for this. Some hire companies do this. They charge more for large or broadcast work, but are prepared to charge less for smaller companies. Some will quote smaller companies the same, because they don't really want the work. There are a few who only have low end equipment and are small themselves and are considerably cheaper. Simon uses Bob because Ace Productions have worked up a good relationship with them and Bob will always provide people who have worked for them before.

Bob is also very fair. He tells Simon that what he could do with one camera in three days, could probably be done in a day and a half with two for this particular shoot. He also points out the fact that it sounds as if Simon is looking at a three-machine edit, in which case he will need two rolls of different masters to get the effects he wants. The alternative is non-linear. He knows some good post production people and will discuss it at the meeting. Simon needs a figure for his budget, but decides to guess from his rate cards. Bob will probably come up with something less expensive, anyway.

He thinks 'an off the top of my head figure', without having a proper brief, three locations, two Beta SPs with operators for a day and a half would be £750. Stock would be extra as would meals and transport. Lighting and sound would not be a problem, but would add £200 per person for the day and a half. He would, of course supply the lights and sound equipment, but not the stock, meals or transport. All the prices are based on a 30 day invoice.

He would like to come to a meeting to get the feel of the programme and, if it was late afternoon and a promise of some refreshment afterwards, he wouldn't charge.

Simon looks at his watch and is quite pleased with this. It has only taken just over an hour and he has got a lot of answers. He now goes back to the Production Plan on his desk and starts to fill it in.

			Simon. Production Plan Page 1.
P. L. V. T.	CONTACT	D/T	RESULT
376281	Mr Hermandes	6/8	*Secretary, H. ringing back. mention video people*
V. (Factory) 0842634891	?		*Unit 14. Wandle Bus Pk. Smithies.*
V. (Des) 643291	?		*21, Gothic Rd.*
6874476201	Julian	6/8	*N/R*
230871ε321	Joe Martin	6/8	*Sally Beagle. Poss 9th pm. JM ringing back*
V. (College)	?		
598406	Bob (Crew)	6/8	*£750 - 2 Beta SP's. £400 sound/light Meeting O.K. Knows Post/Prod people.*
T. (Invoice)			
T. (Budget)			

The storyboard

You will hear and read different things about the storyboard. With drama, particularly, the story may already exist. It is then turned into a screen-play, which has a format similar to a normal play. The director then plans, with the visualization department, how this will be interpreted visually. This is drawn up as the storyboard.

For our purposes the normal sequence of events is to offer the client your treatment and discuss it. Often the treatment will have the sort of images you imagine written into it. Once the treatment has been agreed the next stage is to do the visualization. This becomes the storyboard and has a series of still images drawn in boxes in the video format that the programme will use, this is normally 4:3, but there is a growing tendency towards wide screen format (16:9). Additionally normally at the side, but sometimes underneath, these boxes will be an area for the script.

The boxes will be numbered and these numbers refer to the shot number. The still images are the pictures of the opening shot referring to the shot number, if a shot develops (pans or zooms for example), an instruction to that effect will be written in. Only when the shot changes do we need to draw another image. Sometimes the script is only written as the first and last line, but in this case there should be a full script kept separately, more normally the whole script is written beside each shot, it is often the script which dictates a change of shot. Any music or sound effects are put in a separate column after the script.

The storyboard is the first time that the actual sound and pictures are put together in visual form. It is also the last time, because other documents will now be used that give only sound information or only picture information in the form of a script or camera cards. The storyboard is the last check the client will have before being committed to the expensive process of production.

The storyboard marks a very important stage in the pre production stage. It is not only at this stage that a representation of the actual programme can be seen, but is often the stage at which the client will be expected to pay part of the programme fee.

Minor changes may be made to the programme once the storyboard has been approved, but anything major will involve the client in more money. For this reason alone the storyboard must be an accurate representation of precisely what is going to be seen and heard.

The storyboard is the responsibility of the scriptwriters who will have visualization artists working with them. Very often, because of the obvious differences between a theatre production and a television production, the scriptwriter is known as the screenwriter. Whichever title they use it is important that they are fully aware of the television process and what is, and is not, possible with cameras and, particularly, when to use which size of shot. Although the final decision during production is the director's, the whole programme has to be conceived at this stage as accurately as possible to its finished form.

Obviously a storyboard drawn in full colour with a large number of shots, some representing complex animation and effects, will take artists a considerable time to originate. This will be reflected in the cost. Even a computer graphics generated storyboard takes time, although it is now easier for lesser artists to make the result look like a professional work of art! Some companies use a combination of computer generated artwork, 'real drawings' and even photographs. What you must do with your storyboard is what you think is appropriate and what you can negotiate with the client. Never think you can get away with a few squiggles and a bit of 'Mid shot of Sally' unless you have negotiated this with the client, as Elaine did.

Ace Productions cannot justify the expense, or time, for a fully visualized colour storyboard for this short continuous programme where there is no beginning or end, and therefore no continuous story line. Elaine has agreed with Mr Hermandes that she will do a simplified storyboard. There are degrees of simplification and in this case she has suggested that the sequence of shots will be followed accurately, but she will describe them in words, with the odd 'pin-men' diagram to illustrate a particular point. £250 is a fair price for this and Simon's budget which will take him a couple of hours.

This is one type of storyboard. These can be purchased in A3 size pad form, which saves making your own template. The small disadvantage is that they will need to be folded to go into your production diary.

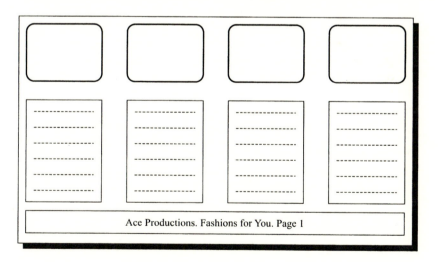

Ace Productions. Fashions for You. Page 1

The other type is simply an A4 sheet with a suitable storyboard grid marked on it. This is the one that Ace Productions uses. There are two reasons; this blank sheet can be stored as a template on their computer so that they can computer generate part, or all, of their storyboard using A4 paper that is already in the printer and it will fit neatly in the production diary in a form where it can be viewed easily through its A4 pocket. Which you use is a matter of preference. As always there is never a right or wrong, merely a 'different'.

We can see how Elaine is getting on by looking at one of her pages. She has to storyboard the programme from beginning to end because it is, in reality, simply a 'normal' programme. What makes it different as a programme is the way the viewer will see it. She agreed the treatment with Mr Hermandes which takes short cameos of the process from design through production to product, with a voice-over used as a link and to reinforce the processes. Because the viewer could pass at any time during these three processes it must be possible to pick up the storyboard at any page and follow say 10 or 15 shots that will show these stages.

You will probably have been given guidelines for shot length and type. Again, with this programme, we will have to break the rules. Elaine will use developing shots that have movement and shot movement, for example she may zoom in slowly to a designer working on a pair of slacks and mix whilst the shot is still zooming in to a zoom out of a model on the catwalk wearing the slacks. This type of shot is used in pop videos but is considered very unconventional in 'normal' programmes.

Editing would be impossible if shots were just cut together in a random order, which is what makes this programme difficult. There has to be some logical sequence to hold the attention of the viewer as long as possible, certainly long enough for them to see all the stages.

You will see that Elaine has got as far as page 6, while Simon was making his phone calls. She has nearly finished. We can see from these six shots that she is staying with the treatment and mixing design with manufacture and the catwalk. She has followed this sequence throughout but, as you will see this sequence goes 'designer, catwalk, manufacture', then back to the catwalk for a different product. She is changing the order to avoid repetition.

You will also notice that she is using the voice-over to link the shots. As agreed in the treatment she is using the company logo as often as possible and is including a small caption for each girl.

		Comments and Script	
Shot 30	Start with MLS of designer (Over shoulder) working on slacks design. Zoom in to design.	'The care taken from concept through to the final design is clear to see. Fashions for You . . .	Music Continues . . . Punchy, Vibrant
Shot 31	*Fashions for You*	*Fades in/out over 5 second mix between shots 30 and 32.*	
Shot 32	Start LS of girl on catwalk in slacks & shirt. Zoom to fill screen with slacks. Girl advances/turns.	are proud of the exciting range of casual trousers and the quality designer look of the final product.'	Mix in applause
Shot 33	making slacks in detail / cat-walk / design	*3 screen (all moving) girl walks back to show reverse of trousers, designer working, main shot is factory. Making slacks. Show detail of stitching.*	Fade out applause
Shot 34	Detail shot (above) continues to zoom out to show the manufacture.		
Shot 35	MS catwalk. Girl in shirt turns. **Linda**	'The latest shirt design is one of the Fashions for You best sellers, and you can see why!' *Fade in/out cap for Linda.*	

Ace Productions – Fashions for You – Trade Show Presenter –   Page 6

This book is about the production diary; you will be taught how to produce a storyboard, so look at the layout Elaine has used. No rights or wrongs, do's or don'ts, Ace Productions use a different typeface for the voice-over and directions, because they are in the same column. This is a simplified storyboard so the shots are not visualized but described. Where she needs to, Elaine has drawn simple pictures, the Fashions for You logo has been changed for visual effect. It may be changed back by the client.

However you decide to do your storyboard it is the final document that will be presented to the client. It can be called upon as a contract, and the programme must follow it. You must keep a copy in the production diary, you must agree it with the client and, to that end, you would be wise to get a signature from the client to say it has been agreed.

It is now nearly half past seven on a Friday night. Elaine is finishing off her storyboard and Simon has been busy starting his budget.

Mr Hermandes rang back to say he had arranged for Simon to meet the designers at Gothic Road on Tuesday morning. The sales director would like to meet him first so it was suggested that they all meet at Mr Hermandes office at 9 o'clock. They could then go on to the factory. The video was no problem, but it would be sensible to chat to the designers and factory staff individually about their 'cameo performance'.

Joe Martin rang back to say the arrangements for Monday night were OK. He would be on duty that evening, and would get some figures by then.

Julian has not rung back.

All of these phone calls are written up on Simon's production plan and the notes he made whilst on the phone are filed with the original phone call notes.

Although he has started thinking about the budget, Simon thinks it would be better to start afresh in the morning, he chats with Elaine and they agree to meet at the office at 8.30 in the morning. Are you prepared to do a hard week's work, finish late on Friday and then come in on Saturday? This is the profession you are thinking of choosing. This is the way it is!

Saturday morning comes and Elaine is going to collate and organize the bits of paper that are accumulating, index, cross reference and copy them to organize the production diary. Simon is starting to get serious about the budget.

Budgets – draft

We have already said there are really three budgets. The client budget is, initially, often a guess based on experience but needs to be derived from the predicted budget when commissioning becomes a reality. The actual budget is made up of the final figures, what the production really cost, which will tell us whether we made a profit (and how much) or not.

As with everything there is no one way of doing a budget. There are several accepted methods which largely depend on the scale of the production. Large production companies will use a specially designed software package, smaller companies will use a simple spreadsheet programme. There are also many layouts that can be adopted and it is essential that you know what needs to be costed. The answer, of course, is everything!

The most commonly used methods section the budget into natural elements of the production. Major productions use headings of 'above the line costs', 'below the line costs' and 'indirect costs'. There are different schools of thought about what is 'above the line' and what is 'below the line'. One suggests that the writing, performing and production elements are 'above the line'. These will include all the costs involving the production personnel (people like the director, scriptwriter, cast and music composer). 'Below the line' are the physical elements involved, things like the technical elements of studio and crew, set designers, transport, sound, lighting, and editing for example.

Another method uses basically the same format but puts the cast 'below the line' and keeps only the key writing and production personnel of producer, director and scriptwriter 'above the line'.

Both suggest that 'indirect costs' are items like legal and insurance fees and overheads. 'Overheads' is often used as a 'catch all' figure. You may decide to put in a figure for contingency purposes, or use it for rent, rates, electricity etc. for your office.

There are situations where a producer will dream up an idea for a drama or soap, for example, or they may find a novel that they think would make a good film or TV programme. This is a very different situation to the small corporate 'Fashions for You' programme we are concerned with. These large scale productions follow a different early pre production stage to the one we are looking at. The first stage on from the idea that 'this would make a good video' is to think about what target audience it would appeal to and the likely cost. The next stage would be to draw up an outline proposal which consists of a development of the idea to sample script level, the target audience and a simplified budget. Rather like Elaine and Simon put in some time (time is money!), as a result of a request for a programme, this large scale production starts life as an idea which then has to be sold to a client. It costs considerably more to get it to the proposal stage, because it involves more specialist staff, and then the producer will go out and 'sell' it to a client, perhaps a commercial TV station.

Some TV stations can be approached directly at the idea stage and will offer development money with no other guarantees. This is similar to Mr Hermandes agreeing to pay for the storyboard and budget. If you decide to use a standard computer model that follows this complex budget, the client will still require a summary sheet similar to the one shown here for 'My idea'.

You may think that it is very complicated, particularly as all the sections will be individually broken down on separate sheets listing each person or item by hours needed and cost per hour. Nothing can be left out. Even a cup of coffee has a price, and if it is not costed in to the budget you will either have to pay for it yourself, or enter into some very tricky and embarrassing negotiations with the financial backers, or client, because you have gone 'over budget'.

Simon needs a model that is more suitable for small scale productions (like the Fashions for You video), and he will use the three areas of pre production, production and post production plus a sheet for indirect costs. The methodology is still the same; there will be four areas on the summary sheet that will be given to the client. Each of these areas will then have its own sheet which is the complete breakdown for that area.

We said that there are really three budgets, the client budget, the predicted budget and the actual budget. Now you can see how these are derived; the client budget is the summary sheet. Originally, as an indication of costs, Simon used his experience and a bit of guess work to come up with a breakdown which went with the treatment. Now he will work out accurately three separate sheets for pre production, production and post production and include one for the indirect costs. These will then be merged into the summary sheet.

To keep track of the budget, so that it does not go over budget, Simon has a separate column for the actual figures next to the predicted figures. It is then simple to see that he might have overestimated one item which gives him a bit of leeway if he has underestimated another.

DRAFT BUDGET for 'MY IDEA'. 25 JUNE 1999

The budget is based on a three week location, four day studio shoot and four weeks of editing and post production.

Producers Fees	£
Directors Fees	£
Scriptwriters Fees	£
Script Fee	£
Development Cost	£

SUB TOTAL £

Salaries for cast	£
Salaries for production crew	£
Salaries for editing and post production crew	£
Graphics fee	£
Music fee	£
Studio rental	£
OB. rental	£
Editing rental	£
Location costs	£
Transport costs	£
Meals and subsistence	£
Video tape cost	£
Sundries and expenses	£

SUB TOTAL £

Accountants and legal fees	£
Overheads	£

SUB TOTAL £

TOTAL £

You cannot allow a situation to develop whereby you get to the end of the production, having never looked at the budget during the programme, only to find you are £1000 over budget. Equally it is very unprofessional to celebrate if you are £1000 under budget. This sort of error means that another producer could have done exactly the same programme for £1000 less. This will, sooner or later, lead to you losing work because you are too expensive.

Yes, budgets are hard and not very interesting but you must treat them with the same respect and diligence as the rest of your programme. Do you still want to be a producer, or would you rather do lighting or camera?

It is Saturday morning. Elaine and Simon are in the office. Elaine is going to check and organize the production diary. Simon is going to start on the draft budget. He hasn't got all the figures he needs, but, working with a spreadsheet program, that doesn't matter, he will guess some of the figures and replace them later.

Julian still hasn't rung back. Elaine will try to get hold of him, or write him a recorded delivery letter.

To arrive at the summary budget sheet for Mr Hermandes, Simon must first work out the cost of each of the elements. He starts with pre production.

Budgets and schedules tend to go hand in hand. If the schedule allows for one day of shooting then the budget will show a cost for that one day. If the shoot isn't completed in a day, time has to be found as well as more money which wasn't allowed for. We will look at schedules later, but notice that there is a 'Days' column in the budget.

The 'Rate' is the day rate or the item cost. You will see the two columns of 'Estimate' and 'Actual' followed by a column for 'Diff' (difference). Simon uses Estimate instead of Predicted. They are the same and which you use is up to you! The Difference column is where he checks if the budget is staying accurate. If, for example, the research takes a whole day, rather than the half day allotted, the actual figure would change to £80 and the difference figure would show up in red (debt) as £40. Savings of £40 now have to be found somewhere to avoid going over budget.

This is not a simple situation. It would be lovely if the savings could be made in the pre production stage, but in reality it may come from post production or have to come out of contingency. The important thing is that you are aware of the situation as it occurs and don't wait till the end of the programme before you fill in the 'Actual' column.

Ace Productions. – Budget – (Estimated v. Actual) – Client Mr Pat Hermandes.

FASHIONS for YOU – VIDEO PRESENTER. BUDGET

BUDGET BREAKDOWN FOR PRE PRODUCTION

ITEM	NOTES	DAYS	RATE	ESTIMATE	ACTUAL	DIFF
Research		0.5	£80.00	£40.00		
Script		0.25	£80.00	£20.00		
Storyboard		0.5	£80.00	£40.00		
Budget		0.5	£80.00	£40.00		
Transport			£60.00	£60.00		
Subsistence			£125.00	£125.00		
Telephone/Mail			£35.00	£35.00		
Location recce		1.5	£100.00	£150.00		
Production Manager		10	£100.00	£1000.00		
Director		10	£100.00	£1000.00		
P.A.		2	£40.00	£80.00		
		Sub Totals £		£2590.00		

page 2

A little like computers crash when you least want them to, budgets will go over when you least expect it! You back up your work on the computer, so take similar care with your budget over (or under) shoots.

Notice something else that is interesting. Both Simon and Elaine (production manager and producer) have charged their time at £100 per day and Simon has allowed ten days of pre production for both of them with a day and a half extra for his location recce. I said earlier that how much you charge is up to you, if you are just starting out it would not be wise to try charging Hollywood money! My experience is that people tend to be famous and then rich, rather than rich and famous.

Further examination shows that the storyboard and budget have both been charged at half a day each, at a day rate of £80. Mr Hermandes will be invoiced £250. Has Simon made a mistake? What Simon has shown is that the storyboard and budget cost £40 each. Someone has got to take the time to construct them. In this case it is Simon and Elaine, who are charging £80 per day for this work, instead of their normal £100. The treatment is the £60 'Research' and 'Script' which has been subtly added in totalling £140. This leaves £110 to cover some of the very early work, and a little profit. The company has to make money too!

Notice, also, that as agreed at the production meeting, Simon has costed in two days for a PA. It may be that the PA will have to go if the budget comes to more than the £8000 Mr Hermandes says he will pay. This is Simon's working sheet. Mr Hermandes will not be given the break-down, only the final figure for pre production of £2590.

Giving the client the breakdown is very silly! Do you want him to say he's not paying £125 for sandwiches for 10 days? Do you want him to know you are charging £60 for transport? Is there anything you would have added, or taken out? Do you think it is fair? Is this a good system to use, or have you got a better one? Nothing is right or wrong – only different.

For the Production breakdown, Simon has allowed 2 days, and has costed in the PA.

You will remember that he does not know what Joe Martin will charge for the use of the facilities, or the girls. He will not know until Monday night, and possibly not then. What he has done is gone back to the last production diary, which involved a day in studio. He sees from the budget sheets that the actual studio cost was just over £2000 for the day. That included all the crew, except make-up, wardrobe, and equipment. The staging and props had to be made and brought in.

If he can use the Genie College theatre facilities they must cost him less. Studio is a controlled environment, and he would save more money by not needing Bob for two days. The break down this sheet shows is that he could afford to pay Joe a maximum of £400 for the facilities and £150 for the girls. He gets this figure by knowing he cannot risk half a day shoot with unknown artists in the uncontrolled environment of Genie College. He will have to ask Bob to supply crew for 2 days, rather than 1½, which will come to £1500. That leaves him £550 as the difference from the studio hire cost.

His last production budget showed that he paid the figures shown for props, staging, wardrobe and make-up so he has simply repeated them. Do you see how useful a previous production diary has been? Simon can be confident that the most he will pay is just over £2000, so if Joe Martin does not come up with figures that match the estimated budget, he goes

Ace Productions. – Budget – (Estimated v. Actual) – Client Mr Pat Hermandes.

FASHIONS for YOU – VIDEO PRESENTER, BUDGET

BUDGET BREAKDOWN FOR PRODUCTION

ITEM	NOTES	DAYS	RATE	ESTIMATE	ACTUAL	DIFF
Director		2	$100.00	$200.00		
Production Manager		2	$100.00	$200.00		
P.A.		2	$40.00	$80.00		
Cast		1	$150.00	$150.00		
Music			$300.00	$300.00		
Graphics			$125.00	$125.00		
Camera Crew		2	$500.00	$1000.00		
Sound		2	$125.00	$250.00		
Lighting		2	$125.00	$250.00		
Staging		0.5	$100.00	$50.00		
Make-up		1	$50.00	$50.00		
Wardrobe		1	$50.00	$50.00		
Location Hire		1	$400.00	$400.00		
Props			$175.00	$175.00		
Transport			$50.00	$50.00		
Subsistence			$130.00	$130.00		
Videotape			$200.00	$200.00		
Telephone			$30.00	$30.00		
Sub Totals £				$3690.00		

to studio. If the figures are lower, he can get the overall figure down. He already has that uncomfortable feeling that this is going to work out at more than the £8000 Mr Hermandes will pay!

Now look at Simon's estimate for post production. You will notice that he has allowed 4 days for himself, Elaine and a PA. He has also put in the voice-over costs. You may think that this should be in production, and you may be right!

Simon prefers to get the voice done last. This is because it is not an 'on camera' artist, but a voice-over that needs to record specific sentences to go with specific pictures. Simon finds that it is easier for the voice-over artist to get the right feel and timing if he is actually recording them whilst watching the pictures. Therefore he does it at the audio dub stage. It is possible to get the script recorded and then try and cut it up and fit it to the right pictures, it just seems to Simon that it is a bit like hard work.

You will see that he has costed off line at £200 a day for 2 days. He has decided that he will do the off line at Ace Productions using the BITC VHS copy. The edit suite cost money and it must earn its money, therefore it is charging for its services!

How does Simon know what the costs are? He hasn't any prices yet. You guessed! He went back to his old production diaries and looked up what he has paid in the past for similar programmes. You can now understand the purpose of keeping accurate diaries and of keeping all the old ones.

Has Simon left anything out? He already has a nasty feeling that this will cost more than the client has money for. Maybe the PA will have to go, or maybe there are savings elsewhere. Because this is a spreadsheet program, the figures can be tinkered with and the overall figure reduced. Before this can happen, Simon must have all the figures entered as accurately as possible, he cannot wait for the college or Bob to tell him how much the final figures will be.

Before we look at the summary sheet there is one final sheet that Simon needs to do. This is the indirect costs sheet. Whether you do one for your programmes or not, look at the headings.

Somewhere in your budget you will have to account for insurance. We will talk about that later; for now believe me that you would be totally insane to consider doing a programme without insurance. Simon's old production diaries show that he normally pays £250 for this and provides the name, address and contact he needs to arrange it.

Ace Productions. – Budget – (Estimated v. Actual) – Client Mr Pat Hermandes.

FASHIONS for YOU – VIDEO BUDGET

BUDGET BREAKDOWN FOR PRODUCTION

ITEM	DAYS	RATE	ESTIMATE	ACTUAL	DIFF
Director	4	$100.00	$400.00		
Production Manager	4	$100.00	$400.00		
P.A.	4	$40.00	$160.00		
Off Line Edit	2	$200.00	$400.00		
On Line Edit	1	$600.00	$600.00		
Special Effects	0.5	$300.00	$150.00		
Voice Over	0.5	$350.00	$175.00		
Audio Dub	0.5	$250.00	$125.00		
Telephone		$15.00	$15.00		
Subsistence		$60.00	$60.00		
Video Stock		$180.00	$180.00		
Transport		$25.00	$25.00		
Sub Totals £			$2690.00		

Similarly Ace Productions will start to issue contracts soon. Although the forms have been originated with the help of their lawyer, Simon automatically sends a copy to be checked. The lawyer only charges £100 to look at them and it is money well spent.

Duplicating, arguably, could go into post production. Simon thinks it is actually something that happens after post production. He always sends the client three copies and whether they realize it or not, they pay for them!

Simon is realizing that he is going to find it very hard to make the £8000 final figure, so he cuts back on his contingency. This is a sort of 'just in case' fund. If the programme does start to go over budget and cannot be brought back, this is the final safety net before you start to pay yourself. A guide would be around 20 per cent of the production cost, which works out at about 12 per cent of the total figure. What you decide to put in is up to you. Your quote will be cheaper if you don't allow anything, but it is a big risk. If you put in silly amounts, in the hope of putting it towards the profit, you will make the budget look very expensive compared with other producers, probably losing the programme. Simon has left out a heading for 'Financial'. Normally he would put £300 down for that because a little of each programme cost goes towards the accountant who does the annual books. This time he knows he cannot afford it.

Ace Productions. – Budget – (Estimated v. Actual) – Client Mr Pat Hermandes.

FASHIONS for YOU – VIDEO BUDGET

BUDGET BREAKDOWN FOR INDIRECT COSTS

ITEM	NOTES	ESTIMATE	ACTUAL	DIFF
Insurance		£250.00		
Legal		£100.00		
Duplication		£30.00		
Contingency		£300.00		
	Sub Totals £	£680.00		page 5

The final page of Simon's draft budget is the summary sheet that will go to Mr H.

On here are the sub totals of the three elements (or stages) of the production and the indirect costs. It is now, when they are all added up, that Simon has confirmation of his fears.

The budget is over £9500 against a promise from Mr Hermandes of £8000. Somewhere Simon needs to cut back by £1500. There is a delicate balance here, a bit like a poker game; does he submit the final figure in the hope that the client really does want the programme and is now committed because of the shortage of time? Can he risk the fact that another producer may have been offered £250 for a storyboard and budget by Thursday, as well? If he does say he can't cut it down and Mr Hermandes reluctantly has to accept it, what does that do for Ace Productions' reputation of 'On Budget and on Time'?

I suggest you try to help Simon go through the options – this could be your budget worry next! If they don't hire a PA that would save £320, but would put extra pressure on himself and Elaine. He cannot cut back on the contingency any more, £300 is less than the PA and really not enough. He cannot cut the insurance. To not offer catering would cause another problem, the crew and cast will simply wander off to the pub, probably never to return!

The solution seems to be in cutting back on his and Elaine's salary. The spreadsheet program is used to recalculate the figures if they charged

---

Ace Productions. – Budget – Client Mr Pat Hermandes.

FASHIONS for YOU – VIDEO BUDGET

BUDGET BREAKDOWN BY ELEMENTS OF PROGRAMME

ITEM	ESTIMATE
Pre Production	£2590.00
Production	£3690.00
Post Production	£2690.00
Indirect Costs	£680.00
Totals £	£9650.00

page 1

£75 per day. He has allowed 16 days each, saving £400 each. This brings the figure down by £800 to £8850. Not enough, and they want to be paid for all their hard work. Simon still has a top figure he will accept from the college in his head, but he won't know the final figure until Monday night, and maybe not then.

We will leave you to solve the budget while Elaine studies the script!

The audio script

Elaine has been having a busy day. She has spent some time organizing the production diary into sections, updating the indexes and making photocopies of items that need cross-referencing.

She finally managed to get hold of Julian. He was very contrite and suggested coming into the office on Monday morning to look at the storyboard and discuss the programme. That way he will be able to arrange the price at the same time. Elaine looks at the diary section of the production diary and sees that both she and Simon are free so suggests 10.00 a.m.

When doing the storyboard yesterday she started to rough out the script. Now she gets the storyboard out of its file in the production diary and lays it out on the table so that she can see all the sheets in the right order. She is familiarizing herself with the programme. Does it look as good in the cold light of day? Are there changes she wants to make to the order or content? Does it flow properly? She moves the last sheet and puts it in front of the first sheet. This will be a continuous programme; does the end join to the beginning? Now she starts at Page 4 and continues through. Does it make sense?

She turns her attention to the script. There are rules about a script and some guidelines. It is most important to realize that the script is complementary to the picture. This is not radio, the pictures show the story, and the locations and script should fill in the detail. Neither is video a book. Long descriptions and details cannot be reread; the script should consist of short phrases or sentences that add to the picture, helping the mood or theme that is being portrayed. What makes home movies so boring is the total lack of understanding of this basic concept, and a constant desire to fill every shot with as many words as possible. It is for good reason that there is a famous expression that 'a picture is worth a thousand words'!

To give you an example of how bad it can get, look back at the story-board diagram on page 73. Look at shot 35 and at the script Elaine has suggested to cover this shot.

Now imagine the same shot and the voice-over saying 'here we can see Linda walking down the catwalk in a shirt, as she turns you will notice how nice she looks'. Both sentences take the same time to say, both would cover the shot. The picture is showing a girl in a mid shot, deliberately chosen to accent the shirt. A caption fades in to credit Linda, and who cares what she looks like – you are supposed to be looking at the shirt! Elaine chose a much more punchy sales line of 'the latest shirt design is one of Fashions for You best sellers, and you can see why!' This complements the picture and reinforces the Fashions for You name, coupling it with a 'must have' feeling (it is one of their best sellers).

Script writing is an art. Specialists make a very healthy living. Maybe you would like to be a scriptwriter? You certainly need to know the whole process of television to succeed. Elaine chose what she wanted to do while doing an English degree and becoming interested in television. Now, having been on a course similar to yours, she prefers the creative side of treatments, writing, storyboards and directing to 'all that technical stuff'.

Simon did a business studies course and then went on the television course; he likes playing with budgets and doing recces and editing. He can't see himself as a director and doesn't have much interest in cameras, sound or lighting, so he is going down the production manager route. He still needs all the skills the course taught him, to understand how video fits together. You will have your favourite sections of your course. You cannot be a one-man band in video – it is a team game. Choose to specialize in what you enjoy most.

Elaine settles down with the computer and starts work using her script template. She finds that it helps to think in sound and picture while she is doing the storyboard, so there are ideas of script written on it. Now she has familiarized herself with the whole story in pictures and word ideas she will look at the storyboard in the right order and try to refine the script.

This will then be transferred to the final storyboard. You may just do the storyboard, and then write the script, or spend ages doing the storyboard in pictures and final script. Elaine finds it easier to use her creativity to think up the sort of pictures and words that make up this draft version and then concentrate on getting it right.

Ace Productions – Fashions for You – SCRIPT –		Page 2	
Shot No.	**Script**	**Instructions**	**Music/SFX**
14	Fashions for You is the truly affordable designer wear for the youth of today	Wait till girl is half way down catwalk. Run over to start of 15	Music continues
15	This exciting range is created by a dedicated team of young designers . . .	Let shot establish (3 secs) then time pace to cover first second of shot 16	Music continues
16	. . . helped by skilled craftsmen, to bring you a range of clothes that the youth of today will find chic and desirable,	Pause ½ sec and continue	Fade down music, mix applause over,
17	(none)		Fade out applause, fade up music
18	(none)		Music continues
19	The Fashions for You range changes with the seasons,	Back time to have shot transition coincide with 'seasons, giving . . .'	Music continues
20	giving today's discerning youth the choice they want at prices they can afford.		Music continues

You will see that Elaine has four columns for Shot number, Script, Instructions and Music/SFX (sound effects).

You will notice that she often uses the script to cover a shot transition; this helps the programme to flow. It looks and sounds very odd to have a few words with a picture, a change of picture and a few more words, and so on. This is another 'home movies' fault!

Notice also how she has picked up the Fashions for You key selling points, and tried to use phrases that will help to stop buyers walking straight past. The pictures are going to be busy and fast moving, the script is quietly filling in the gaps, pointing out details and suggesting this is a designer range the buyer must have.

While Elaine has been altering her script, she has been looking at the shots on the storyboard; she is imagining the length and content and 'hearing' the sound that will go with them. She has only slightly changed her original script, a word here, a change of order there.

Remember that Elaine will direct this programme. The more she runs through it now, on paper, and the more she can become familiar with the visualization, the easier it will be for her to get the shots she needs. This will save time and avoid the need for reshoots. She is already learning the programme so she will know what will cut with what when they get to the shooting stage.

Let's see what has happened so far. Ace Productions got a request for a programme by letter on July 8. This resulted in a client meeting, a treatment and an outline budget, some hard negotiating, lots of phone calls, a full storyboard and a full draft budget. It is now August 7.

In the month that this programme has taken so far, the production diary is filling up nicely, which has taken time and a lot of care. All of this for an agreed fee of £250, split between two people and an expensive office.

All of this development work has not been charged because that is the way it is done with small companies trying to get as much work as possible to survive. Realistically Ace Productions has done well to get this far. Other companies were asked to supply treatments and outline budgets only to be sent away with nothing. This is the reality of business. Ace Productions will not know until next week whether they have got this programme or not. Before that they have arranged three location recces and a meeting with their musician. There must be easier ways of making money! You need to really want to work in this business; you will have long hours, a terrible social life and no money until you become established. Remember 'famous then rich'!

Health and safety

While Simon and Elaine take Sunday off, we can look at health and safety matters. Working in the media business means working in a potentially very dangerous place. Lights have exploded or fallen on people. Many a trailing cable has led to a spell on crutches. Scenery has fallen on performers. Electricians have been electrocuted. The list is endless.

All these accidents are treated as 'incidents' by the legal profession and companies do get sued, sometimes for large amounts of money.

All of this has led to many governments around the world passing laws relating to health and safety, meaning that there is a strong possibility that, as well as getting sued, you risk breaking the law and ending up in court.

I am not going to outline the various laws and their implications, but I am going to try to simplify it all and keep it to the practical things that you can do to keep out of trouble.

The legislation applies equally to all employers and employees. Employers are responsible for providing a safe and healthy working environment. This means that equipment must be safe, or have notices attached warning of potential dangers. This 'equipment' includes trailing cables leading from it. There must be adequate, well marked, fire exits with a totally clear safety lane leading to them. The exits and safety lane must be lit at all times and stay alight in the event of electrical failure.

Employers are also responsible for the health and welfare of their staff. This means that if a member of your crew is unfit through illness, flu for example, it is your responsibility to replace them. Welfare includes things like providing sensible working hours with scheduled breaks for meals.

Gone are the days when you can drag the cameraperson out of hospital and work them for 24 hours with no break!

It is the duty of employees to take reasonable care of their own health and safety and other people who may be affected by their actions. To take a simple example, an employer has to make sure that the ladder and support system for a suspended light are safe and pose no risk to a qualified electrician. The qualified electrician who fits the light is responsible for ensuring that it is safe and secure and neither it, nor its connections and cables, pose any risk to anybody, including members of the public.

In a short sentence, everybody has a duty of care to themselves and everybody else.

Companies, by law, have to draw up a health and safety at work policy, have health and safety committees and have regular training for staff, in addition they must keep an accident book that is open to inspection by the Health and Safety at Work inspectors. They must also carry out regular risk assessment to highlight the areas of risk and the degree of risk involved. Health and safety is a very serious matter.

Generally speaking it is the production manager who is responsible for the health and safety aspects of the production. Simon does this job for Ace Productions and he likes to do a risk assessment when he does his recce. This means that he will look for potential or actual dangers that may become an issue when shooting starts. This could include something as simple as noticing a container of cleaning fluid that could be knocked off a shelf, or as complicated as checking that there is enough power in the building to drive all the equipment he needs.

I am not going to start an electricity lesson, but suffice it to say that four 13 amp sockets in one room does not necessarily mean that you have 52 amps to play with, nor does it mean that you can 'Christmas tree' a socket with lots of multiple adapters.

Monday morning has arrived. Elaine and Simon have an impromptu production meeting over their first cup of coffee. This does not need to be minuted and go into the production diary, because Elaine is checking the stage they are at and is going to draw up an agenda for the Wednesday morning meeting. They look at the storyboard and draft budget, realize that they have problems, but agree to talk about it at the meeting. They will both see Julian at 10.00 a.m. after which Simon will check the video camera and the paperwork he needs to take to Genie College tonight.

Julian arrives late, bringing an extended piece of music with him as a sort of offer of apology. He agrees that he isn't very reliable but assures them that the music will definitely be done within a week of them commissioning him. He studies the storyboard and is impressed. He, too, now has a feel for the programme and that helps him. They play the music while watching the shots and agree it would definitely enhance the programme. He thinks about £200 would be a good guess. Simon says a guess is not good enough because the figure will go into the contract. Julian says he will settle for £200.

The recce (1)

Recce is the industry shorthand for reconnoitre. This involves thoroughly examining the location, drawing up plans and checking what facilities are available. It helps if an electrician can be present, perhaps a member of the lighting team, if you are unsure of power supplies and loading. Apart from suitability, one purpose of the recce is to find out what problems may occur whilst actually shooting at this location.

The questions that need answering fall into two categories: physical and physiological. The physical questions that need answers should be drawn up as a scale plan. What is needed is a set of diagrams similar to studio plans, but they must be created for each location. A few typical questions that will help provide the details are: How big is the space? How high is the ceiling? Where are the doors/windows? Which direction does the window face? What colour is the wall/ceiling? What is the available light? From where? How many power sockets are there? What sort are they and how much current is available? What obstructions are there? (A large signpost, or a parking meter, may need to be 'camouflaged' by a horse and cart in a period drama, or a removal van in modern settings.) What access is available for people, vehicles and equipment? Particularly helpful to the sound team will be, what is the level of ambient noise? What type of noise? (Obvious disasters occur when nobody noticed the church clock that strikes on the quarter hour, or the fact that the room is immediately opposite the fire station.) Where are the fire exits and is the safety lane clearly marked?

Some physiological questions concern the well being of the crew and performers. Again, examples would be: Is there somewhere discreet for performers to change/make-up? Where are the nearest toilets? Where is the nearest place for refreshments (or do you need to make arrangements for location catering)? Where is the nearest telephone? How do crew/performers get to the location (draw them a map, or arrange transport)? What are the contact name and telephone number?

It is from these recce plans and notes that the director and crew can work out shots, camera positions, types and number of lights and lighting positions, the sound requirements and foresee any problems that may occur. With small scale programmes, notes and plans may be sufficient. For larger scale programmes, photographs or actual video footage often supplement the notes and plans. Simon always takes his Hi8 for just this purpose; it allows him to try out actual shots and angles.

An example of bad management would be if you decide to take a crew on a shoot in the park, that you think you know because that is where you have your lunch, without thoroughly researching it. Everybody will have a lovely time running about waving a video camera at anything that moves until your time, or the tape, runs out!

Simon has a checklist that he always takes with him so that he doesn't forget anything. He supplements this with shots on his Hi8 that give an overall impression of the location and shots of any particular problems he has noticed. He uses the soundtrack as a useful voice memo pad. This gives him a chance to note things that he might otherwise forget and also gives an impression of the acoustic quality of the location. He makes sure that he leaves some time as 'silence' to judge the ambient sound level and type.

You may benefit from the lesson learnt by Ace Productions about a year ago. They had done a programme for a company and were now doing a six month update. Simon got all the recce notes and plans out of the original production diary and copied them into the new one. When they turned up at the location the walls had been painted a lurid green, the office had become open plan, and they had built on the car park! Never trust anything, go and see for yourself.

Simon has called up his recce template off the computer and is printing it out.

This is not the definitive recce sheet – it is the one Ace Productions use. You may have a completely different one. What you will find interesting is the content. Apart from the usual client and contact names, addresses and phone numbers, you will see a reference to the shots the location will be used for. Simon does this because he will have to look at the storyboard to find the answer and this will familiarize him with the type and content of the shot. He will go to the location with an idea of what he needs in his head.

Videos frequently start with a long shot so that we have a clear perspective of where we are and where everybody is. Simon has a line for 'first impressions'. This is his long shot view before he starts to examine the location in detail. He may think 'this is going to be impossible', or 'that column in the middle of the room is a problem'.

Where the doors are will be on the plan he will draw. Crucial, though, is can the equipment be brought through the door, hence 'Door access size' and 'problems'.

The wall and ceiling colour may affect the shots. Predominantly blue or green will make them look cold or nauseous. Pink or red will warm

Ace Productions. Recce for .... Date.....................................

Client Name .... Phone No ....

Exact Location ....

Location Contact Name ....Phone No ....

To be used for Shot Nos. ....

Parking ....Access ....

First Impressions ....

Length .... Width .... Height ....

Door Access Size .... Problems ....

Window Size .... Problems .... Direction ....

Electric Sockets or Battery Power required ....

No of Sockets ....Type .... Power Available .... Notes ....

Wall Colour ....Ceiling Colour ....Problems ....

Fire Exits .. Yes/No.. Number .... Safety Lane .. Yes/No .. Extinguishers .. Yes/No ....

Sound Problems ....

Lighting Problems ....

Camera Problems ....

Crew Problems ....

Toilets .. Male .... Female ....

Refreshment Area ....

Changing/Make-up Area ....

Incoming Telephone Available .. Yes/No ..... Number ....

Notes ....

....

....

....

....

....

....

....

....

Recce Done by   **What have I forgotten?**

them up a little. This will affect the number and type of lights and probably the position of the performers.

With health, safety and welfare in mind he will check the fire exits and safety lane, the toilet facilities, if there is a separate area for breaks, and what the arrangements are for changing and make-up.

Finally you will note that Simon knows the more recces you do the easier is it to forget something. He always puts the question 'what have I forgotten' next to his signature. He knows it takes a couple of minutes to have a final look around, but might take two hours on shoot day to put something right he forgot.

We will see a completed form when he gets back from his three recces.

Simon now prepares his location checklist. Again he has a prepared template on the computer. To appear relaxed and professional when you are meeting people for the first time, you must be well prepared. It is not good news to say 'have you got a pen I could borrow', or start writing notes on the back of a cigarette packet. Pilots take off many times a week, but they still have a checklist that they work through before they do it. It isn't they can't remember, it is that they do it so often they could easily leave something out. So could you and Simon.

You will see that Simon has been able to fill in some of his checklist. You will notice that the Ace Productions standards of professionalism are carried though to everything. The car must be clean and tidy, as must Simon. He will take two recce forms, pens and pencils, just in case. He will take spares for the Hi8.

You will also have spotted Simon's personal trick of making himself double check everything. He has put 'what have I forgotten' after his signature completing the list.

You may think that all of this preparation is a little unnecessary. You may be right. This is the way Ace Productions does it; it is not the way everybody does it. Simon and Elaine have learnt the hard way that only if you have everything covered will it ensure that everything goes smoothly. The last thing you need when you come to the actual shooting is problems that will cost time and money. The pre production side is key to the whole programme. That is why it takes so long, and must be done thoroughly.

Are you beginning to realize that if you want to just go out and have a lovely time waving a camera about, you are committing yourself to a very expensive hobby and will never work in the video business?

Ace Productions – Recce Check list for: *Fashions for You - Factory*

Date   *10th August 99*   Time   *p.m.*

Address   *Unit 14, Wandle Bus Pk.*   Phone No.   *0842634899*
                    Smithies

Contact   Phone No.

Special arrangements?   *Meet Mr H at 21 Gothic Road 9 a.m.*

CAR

Washed?   Vacuumed?   Petrol?   Parking money?

ME

Neat and tidy?   Clip Board?   2 Pens?   2 Pencils?

A4 Note Pad?   Tape measure?   2 Recce Forms?

Notes?

EQUIPMENT

Hi8   Charged battery   Spare charged?

Videotape loaded?   Spare videotape?

On camera light?   Spare bulb?

Test Shots done?

Check List Complete?   **What have I forgotten?**

Supplier meetings

Simon has filled in his checklist for Genie College and goes to meet Joe Martin. If Ace Productions get this programme, which they are confident of doing because it is dependent only on budget and storyboard, Joe Martin will become a supplier. He will provide Simon with services or goods that will be paid for. As such, contracts and model release forms will have to be issued. The health and safety of the college's girls will be Ace Productions' responsibility. This visit has two purposes – one is the recce, the other is a supplier meeting.

There has already been a supplier meeting with Julian. Things were agreed, prices were fixed, dates were promised. With Julian that was all relatively simple, they have worked together before, know each other as friends and, apart from Julian's unreliability, they respect each other professionally. This meeting is different; Simon has never met Joe.

The important thing about this meeting is that Simon has to be in charge. It is his programme; he can shoot it where he likes and use whomever he pleases as performers. It is too easy to allow a programme to be taken over by enthusiasm. Joe obviously wants it shot in his theatre, using his girls. It is good publicity for his department and the college. Simon knows what he is prepared to pay, he doesn't know if the facilities or the girls are suitable. He will not allow himself to be bullied into doing something he isn't happy with. He will not commit to an evening shoot because he does not have the budget for crew overtime. If it isn't right, it isn't right and that is that.

Simon meets Joe in his office. He explains that they are 99 per cent certain of getting the programme, but that it is dependent on the budget, which is being a bit of a problem at the moment. It is nothing to do with Joe what the budget is, it would be a breach of confidentiality to tell him. Simon simply wants Joe to know that if he is thinking up Hollywood figures for the use of the college, he can forget it. Previous negotiations have taught Simon that if a supplier wants something badly enough he will lower the price to get it.

Joe suggests they look at the facilities and meet the girls. Simon decides that there is no point in doing that unless the price is right. He steers Joe towards a price. *'Before we move out of the office, can you give me an indication of price? We would need the facilities and the girls for one day in three weeks' time. I can give you the date when we have scheduled the shooting. Additionally we cannot afford the overtime involved in an evening shoot.'*

This is assertive. Simon is showing he is in charge. The price is more important than the facilities, he is paying for it and it will be shot when he says.

Joe tries the 'how much have you got', technique, Simon says that he has already mentioned that the budget is tight and that the alternative would be a studio, with all its facilities and advantages. He concedes that the studio would cost him about £1500 in total. That includes the crew, make-up, wardrobe and changing facilities. This is a negotiating ploy of Simon's, he is now the client, and Joe has to come up with something suitable. You know that Simon allowed £2000 maximum, but he needs to cut the budget and he certainly is not going to offer it. He does, however, have to be fair.

Joe suggests that the principal thinks that £250 for the hire of the theatre for a day would be fair. It would not include lighting, sound or stage people, that is Joe's responsibility. Simon looks at his notes and sees that he allowed £400 for the cost of the location. He does not show his excitement at this lower figure but continues his negotiations.

'It would make sense for us to use your lights with our operator, video lighting is different to theatre lighting and time would be critical. We obviously need someone to do make-up and wardrobe, and we would need some staging built and dressed. What would that come to as a package, including the personnel?'

Joe has obviously thought this one out in advance, because he says *'I have talked to our backstage crew course and they would love to be involved. They could build a stage and catwalk, Sally wants to teach the make-up people the difference between theatre and video make-up and wardrobe would be happy to help the girls. We did put on a fashion show at Christmas for the fashion department so they already have some experience. Would it be possible for the second year people to be the audience? Everybody wants to get involved, you see.'*

Simon is beginning to think this is sounding very good. He has yet to see the facilities and he knows he must keep a tight rein on 'onlookers'. *'We would need some audience, but we wouldn't pay them, the fewer people we have, the easier it is to control and we are shooting a professional programme for a client. How much are we talking about for a package with you supplying the facilities, lighting, staging and crew?'*

Joe says he has come up with a figure of £450, which would include the facilities, building the sets and the make-up and wardrobe people. That is dependent on Simon allowing as many of the course as practically possible to watch. He also says that he has had a word with the canteen manager who would be happy to provide sandwiches, coffee and juice for the day at what Joe thinks is a very reasonable £60.

Simon asks about the girls. Joe explains that he cannot employ them directly, that would be something that Simon would have to negotiate with them individually. His suggestion is to offer three girls £40 each.

Simon has been very busy writing all this down, it will form part of a contract.

'Shall we go and have a look at the facilities? I know Sally and the girls are waiting to show you round.' Joe leads Simon out of the office and down to the theatre. On the way Simon gets permission to try out a few shots on his Hi8.

Simon has conducted this meeting professionally and fairly. He has asserted himself, given nothing away about how much he could actually afford, and consequently he knows he can cut the budget, but will it be enough?

He does his recce, fills in the sheets, draws his plans, does some test shots showing the facilities and he has taken some footage of the girls. He has been very careful to promise nothing to the girls. He has explained that they will need three, he cannot say which three because the client may have ideas about height, size and looks.

It is late; he politely refuses the offer of a quick drink and goes home. Why do you think he refused a drink? Would you have gone? Would you have then compromised your position of being the client and them the supplier? Would you have been trapped into saying or promising too much as the drinks flowed? Can you stay in charge and assertive with your suppliers when you socialize with them? Look what's happened with Julian. He has become very unreliable and difficult to control because Simon does go for a drink with him.

The recce (2)

It is 9.00 a.m. on Tuesday morning and Simon, having completed his recce check forms, and got everything with him, is with Mr Hermandes and the sales director, who has been introduced as Naomi Findler.

The sales director hopes that everything is going well, she very much likes the treatment and hopes that the budget can be brought into line with the agreed figure. Simon says that they very much want to do the programme and that he is confident that it will. The sales director explains that it is sales budget that is paying for the programme, Mr Hermandes is overseeing the project from the Fashions for You point of view but she must take any decisions. Now we know whom the client is!

She suggests that, because of the time frame, Elaine should bring the budget and storyboard to her office on Thursday morning at 9 a.m. She can then make a decision while Elaine is there.

Simon explains about the possible use of Genie College and shows them the shots he got last night. The sales director says that she wants a size 10 and two size 12 girls, she also likes the idea of the link with the local college. She will consult her staff and put together a package of the clothes they would like used. She also adds that perhaps the girls would like to keep them, as a thank you for their trouble.

Simon is very encouraged by all this. He has got some important decisions resolved already and he has a feeling that the programme is already theirs, if he can meet the budget.

He and Mr Hermandes go to meet the designers. Simon is worried about the location, he doesn't tell Mr Hermandes but his first impressions are of a long thin design office surrounded on three sides by glass. The ceiling is no more than 2½ metres and the only good news is that what there is of the walls and ceiling are cream.

There is a fire exit at both ends, but no defined safety lane; you would have to weave your way around desks. There isn't a fire extinguisher in sight! There are dozens of power points, but he suspects they are on the same ring main.

He asks about the toilets, and whether there is a refreshment area they can use. Mr Hermandes says he will come to see 'what's going on' (probably out of curiosity) while they are shooting, but while they are here Miss Linda Swallow, the chief designer, is in charge. Simon gets the extension number.

Simon paces out the room and measures the door. He suggests they have a quick chat in Miss Swallow's office. He asks who would like to be in the video and can he try out a few shots.

Miss Swallow has already talked to the designers and several have volunteered. They are invited into the office and Simon explains that he can only use four people. The details have not yet been worked out, but they will be shown working on the designs for the clothes that will be shown being made in the factory. He also asks if it would be possible to group those people together for the shoot, by a window wall. Why do you think he asked that? What difference does it make where they are working? They all have their own desks and drawing boards and they are all the same. Is he being awkward? He explains *'It will be easier for us, and cause least disruption to you, if the people we use are together. That way we can set up lighting and cameras to cover one small area causing the least disturbance to everyone else. It will save us having to move lights, camera and crew to what would effectively be a new location each time.'* Did you think of that?

He also wants space around them, which may mean moving some of the other desks. He needs this arrangement to allow the crew to set up lights and work in as much space as possible.

He has noticed that one side faces north and the other south. He would prefer it if the group could be on the north side of the room. Why do you think he chose north? Why not in the middle of the room? Are you as thorough as this with the detail when you do your recces, or do you 'turn up and work it out' wasting valuable shooting time? Why do a recce if you are going to leave essential details out? Simon has decided to use the available light, rather than try to get rid of it. This shoot will take most of the morning. He has got enough problems already without having to start fighting shadows, and great chunks of moving light as the sun moves from east to south, while they are shooting. Better to use a shadowless north light. Did you think of that?

Miss Swallow will decide who will be used. Meanwhile, Simon starts taking shots with his Hi8. He needs to try the over the shoulder shot. It will mean quite a high angle. He knows that this is the same time of day that they will be shooting; it is an ideal moment to see the problems with the light.

The maintenance supervisor has turned up. He knows about the electrical sockets. He confirms that they are all on a ring main, but that it is a standard industrial 60 amp ring. This solves the lighting problem. Do you know what a ring main is? Do you know why a 60 amp ring is good news? You need to if you are going to do location shoots. This isn't a book about electricity, so you will have to find out from your lecturer!

Simon and Mr Hermandes go on to the factory. Simon goes through his recce form again. As they leave Simon suggests they go to a local coffee shop. Mr Hermandes agrees. Why does Simon want to take Mr H for a coffee? Can you see the big difference between the college and Mr H? He turned down the offer of a drink with Joe and Sally at the college.

Simon is dealing with a client here, not a supplier. He needs to have a relationship with a client, as well as appearing professional, he needs to see how Mr Hermandes thinks it is all going so far. What better way than an informal chat over a coffee?

Simon will keep the receipt for the petty cash form in the production diary, and enter it in as subsistence. Did you remember that you are supposed to be keeping all the receipts?

Mr Hermandes says he is very impressed with Ace Productions' thoroughness and commitment. He feels that they have put in an awful lot of work so far, and has been glad to have the opportunity of seeing how every little detail is covered. He lets slip, confidentially, that they have already decided to use Ace Productions, but, no matter how he has tried to argue the case with the director, they cannot let the budget go over by more than £300.

Simon has got what he wants. A client who is impressed, confident with his supplier, and a promise of the programme provided he stays within a £300 margin. All this for the price of a cup of coffee and a bun! Simon and Elaine make a good team don't they?

By the time he has dropped Mr H back at Gothic Road and got back to the office it is nearly six in the evening. Elaine has been working on the agenda for the meeting at 8 a.m. tomorrow. Bob has agreed to come because Elaine had a phone call from Simon to say he felt they had got the programme. They have a brief chat about the day and agree that Simon will settle down to sort out the budget while Elaine looks through the video to familiarize herself with the locations. She will find the soundtrack with Simon describing them very helpful, as well as the detail in his notes. She will then photocopy them for the meeting in the morning before she files them all carefully in the production diary.

It is going to be a long evening, but it is worth it. It now depends on Simon and his budget. Elaine looks at one of Simon's recce notes, the factory contact name, address and phone number must be added to the 'Contacts file' in the production diary. This is how the diary builds into a logical order. The recce form will be filed in 'Locations' but some of the information must be transferred elsewhere.

Ace Productions – Recce for *Fashions for You*........ Date..*10/8/99 p.m.*

Client Name ..*Mr Hermandes*............. Phone No .... *376281* ....

Exact Location .... *Factory - Unit 14 Wandle Bus Pk. - Smithies.* ....

Location Contact Name.*Linda Swallow*..Phone No .... *0842634899 Ext. 214* ....

To be used for Shot Nos. .*2, 7, 9, 12, 15, 19, 24, 27, 30/31,33, 42/3, 47*..............

Parking ...*Staff car park (permits needed)* ....Access .. *No problems* ....

First Impressions... *Long & thin. Lots Of windows, desks too close together* ....

Length ... *15m* .... Width .... *4m* .... Height ..... *2.5m* ....

Door Access Size .... *1m x 2m* .... Problems .... *1st floor, no lift.*..................

Window Size ... *Whole wall* .. Problems .. *Ambient light!!* ... Direction.. *N & S* ....

Electric Sockets or Battery Power required .... *Mains* ....

No of Sockets .. *14* ..Type .. *13 Amp.*.. Power Available .. *60Amp.*..Notes..*Ring Main* ....

Wall Colour .... *Cream* ...Ceiling Colour ..... *Cream* .....Problems ..... *Low ceiling* ....

Fire Exits ..Yes/No *Y*.. Number .. *2.* Safety Lane .Yes/No .*N* . Extinguishers. Yes/No *N*..........

Sound Problems.. *None, might mix in a bit of ambient with V/O* ....

Lighting Problems.. *All window - balance for daylight - low ceiling - Cables!*

Camera Problems .. *Space - Height -* ....

Crew Problems .... *Space and movement restricted* ....

Toilets .. Male.. *2 - East end* .... Female .... *2 - West end* ....

Refreshment Area.. *Can use small office - No smoking - Take Bin bags* ....

Changing/Make-up Area .... *Not required* ....

Incoming Telephone Available .. Yes/No . *Y*. Number *0842634899 Ext. 214*....................

Notes..*Tape down cables, Secure lights, check extinguishers* ....

Recce Done by *Simon*   **What have I forgotten?** *Locate main fuses!!*

The final budget

You will remember that the budget is currently some £1500 over target. Simon has got the final figures, from Julian and the college, and now has to see how he can incorporate them to bring the budget down. Elaine has his notes from his meeting with Joe Martin, to file in the production diary under 'Meetings'. He gets out his photocopy.

Meeting with Joe Martin - Genie College - 9 August 99

1. Budget. Facilities £250. I suggest package to include lighting, makeup, wardrobe, staging.

2. Joe wants to involve everybody! I agree that we could use some 2nd year students as audience if the package is right.

3. Joe comes up with package price £450 to cover all above, plus build the catwalk.

3. Canteen will provide food for £60

4. We pay 3 girls £40 each

5. We decide shoot date

Simon gets to work on his budget spreadsheet. The first thing he will do is to modify the production budget. Having visited the locations with his Hi8 he seriously doubts the need for a sound operator. The whole audio track is music; he has got lots of ambient sound (buzz track is the more usual name). Applause (from a CD) and the buzz track can be mixed in at the post production stage. Let's see how far he has got.

Simon knows that the production budget is his working document; the client will not see it. To remind him of what he has done, he has used

Ace Productions. – Budget – (Estimated v. Actual) – Client Mr Pat Hermandes.

FASHIONS for YOU – VIDEO PRESENTER. BUDGET

BUDGET BREAKDOWN FOR PRODUCTION

ITEM	NOTES	DAYS	RATE	ESTIMATE	ACTUAL	DIFF
Director		2	$100.00	$200.00		
Production Manager		2	$100.00	$200.00		
P.A.		2	$40.00	$80.00		
Cast	Modified	1	$150.00	$120.00		
Music	Modified		$300.00	$200.00		
Graphics			$125.00	$125.00		
Camera Crew	1 day 1 – 2 Day 2	2	$500.00	$750.00		
Sound	Not needed	2	$125.00			
Lighting		2	$125.00	$250.00		
Staging	Now included in	0.5	$100.00			
Make-up	location hire	1	$50.00			
Wardrobe	at college	1	$50.00			
Location Hire		1	$400.00	$450.00		
Props	Reduced		$175.00	$100.00		
Transport			$50.00	$50.00		
Subsistence			$130.00	$100.00		
Videotape	Modified		$200.00	$200.00		
Telephone			$30.00	$30.00		
Sub Totals $				$2855.00		

the notes column. You will notice that he has left the days estimated and the day rate alone. This is because, if he comes back to this budget during future programmes he will be able to see how it was modified.

By cutting back on the cast, music, props and subsistence, deciding not to employ a sound person and using Joe's package he has got the figure down by about £800. Not enough, but a good start.

He wants to leave his and Elaine's rate alone, if at all possible, and he wants to keep the PA. You might feel that it isn't worth dropping the PA, just to save £80, but the only way of reducing a budget is to take lots of little bits out. Simon put this budget together with realistic figures, there was no 'let's put in £1500 for me' in this. The figures are what the programme will actually cost. If you modify it recklessly, to bring the overall figure down, you will end up with estimate and actual figures so far apart even contingency won't cover it!

Simon looks at post production. He will cut the off line cost. We said it is him that is doing it and this is the equipment cost. He doesn't like it but he cuts it in half to £200.

He is now down to £8615. He cannot cut the last £400 from indirect costs. There is no way this programme is being done without insurance, the lawyer must see the contracts and he has left contingency lower than he would like.

He has to make cuts in pre production. He will have some explaining to do to Elaine; he has no choice but to cut their day rate to £80. That is a loss to them of £200 each, and they are earning precious little already. This is the most difficult decision of all to make with a budget. How badly do you want the programme, balanced against how much do you need to survive? He prepares Mr Hermandes' budget breakdown sheet.

It is very late. Simon notices that Elaine has laid out the table for tomorrow's meeting. He picks up the agenda while Elaine photocopies the revised budget.

Ace Productions. – Budget – Client Mr Pat Hermandes.

FASHIONS for YOU – VIDEO PRESENTER. BUDGET

BUDGET BREAKDOWN BY ELEMENTS OF PROGRAMME

ITEM	ESTIMATE
Pre Production	£2190.00
Production	£2855.00
Post Production	£2490.00
Indirect Cost	£680.00
Sub Totals £	£8215.00

page 1

Fashions for You

Production Meeting   8 a.m. 11th August 1999   Elaine, Simon & Bob

AGENDA

1. Programme outline for Bob. – Elaine
2. Recce Gothic College. 9th Aug. (Plans & Notes enclosed) – Simon
3. Recce Design studio. 10th Aug. (Plans & Notes enclosed) – Simon
4. Recce Factory. 10th Aug. (Plans & Notes enclosed) – Simon
5. Shooting requirements. – Simon
6. Post Production ideas. – Bob
Thanks to Bob
7. Budget. – Simon
8. Mr H meeting tomorrow. – Elaine
9. Schedule. (Deferred from last meeting)
10. Contracts.
11. Matters Arising.
12. A.O.B.
13. Date/Time of next meeting.

This meeting is scheduled for no more than 2 hours.

More meetings and phone calls

<u>*Wednesday 11th August 1999. 8 a.m. – Pre production meeting*</u>

This is the heading on the notepad Elaine is using to compile the notes for the minutes of this meeting. You will see four things that are different to the last agenda.

Items 1 to 8 have got names at the end. This indicates that this item will be introduced by the specified person. The chair person will say 'can we move to Item 4 – Simon, please'.

After Item 6 there is an italicized *'Thanks to Bob'*. This indicates the point at which Bob (who is a guest at the meeting), is expected to leave. The remaining items are nothing to do with him. He is a supplier and is providing the crew. He has agreed to come to the meeting and discuss the shooting aspect, but items 7 to 13 are not his business. It is polite, and correct, to indicate on the agenda when he is expected to leave.

Item 7 (Budget) does not say 'attached'. This is because Simon will introduce the budget and hand Elaine the sheets she needs as part of the discussion.

Item 11 is also new. At the last meeting anything that came up was discussed under any other business. This is actually incorrect. AOB should be used to bring up something that has been left off the agenda. Matters arising is the correct agenda item for things that have cropped up during the meeting.

If Elaine was being absolutely correct, Item 1 should be 'Minutes of last meeting'. This is the opportunity for the members of the meeting to agree that the minutes are 'a true and accurate record of proceedings'. Something someone said is easily forgotten, or misunderstood, so it is a sensible agenda item for large meetings. Rather than sit in on the meeting for two hours, let's just read Elaine's minutes.

You can see that problems have arisen, Bob is none too happy that his original estimate of crew members, days and price have been changed. He wants another £100. He is now going to charge for the stock, probably at a higher price than Ace Productions would normally pay, but will include the transport costs. He has also defined the times of the day rate. In the past there has been a fluid arrangement if the shoot overruns by half an hour or so on one day and under the next. Now he will charge for the overrun at double time.

Fashions for You

Production Meeting   8 a.m. 11th August 1999   Elaine, Simon & Bob

MINUTES

1. Elaine described the programme outline to bring Bob up to speed with the types of shot that will be used. The three locations were mentioned. It was suggested that a day would be spent at the two Fashions for You locations and a day at the College. Simon suggested that Bob leave his queries until Item 5.

2. Simon went through the recce plans and notes for the location and ran the video of the location. No problems arose.

3. As 2. above.

4. As 2. above.

5. Simon explained that because of severe budget restrictions he has decided not to use a sound person. Any buzz track would come from an on camera mike or his own track. For the same reason he has decided to use one camera for the Fashions for You locations and two for the College. The shoot would be mastered on Beta SP. He would require a lighting person, and lights, for F for U, but had agreed to use the College lighting rig for that location. This results in a budget figure of £750 for the camera crew and £250 for lighting, which he would like to agree with Bob. Bob said that the original figures were as low as he could go and some minutes of negotiations took place. An agreement was reached at £1100, to include the transport costs, Bob will supply the stock and charge it at cost. Bob needs the shooting dates by the end of the week. Simon asked Bob if the crew could meet at Ace Productions at 8 a.m. on the 2 days required. This was agreed together with a 6 p.m. get out time. Anything over that would be charged at double time.

6. Bob had asked a couple of small companies about the post production. Both could provide audio dubbing facilities. One uses a 3 machine SP suite and digital effects, the other has a mid range non linear suite, which Bob feels would be of suitable quality for VHS copies. Neither would discuss prices, but both said they were competitive in the corporate sector. Bob gave Elaine the contact names and phone numbers. Bob was thanked for all his time and trouble and was assured that contact would be made within a couple of days. Elaine asked if she could have the recce notes and plans back. Bob left.

Fashions for You

Production Meeting   8 a.m. 11th August 1999   Elaine, Simon & Bob

MINUTES

7. Simon introduced the amended budget. A decision has to be made in view of the fact that it cannot be reduced further without the programme becoming uneconomical. Because of Item 5 they are now an extra £100 over budget and have yet to confirm the Post Production figure. Elaine wants it put on record that she is unhappy about the drop in the day rate for Pre Production and Off Line, but has to accept the situation. Simon wants it put on record that his original estimate, which Elaine took to Mr H., was £10,000 and it was her that agreed a top figure of £8000. His feeling is that they should not have proceeded beyond that point. Simon will contact the Post Production facilities after the meeting and discuss prices. Simon agreed that he had not done an invoice for Mr H. and would do so after the meeting.

8. Elaine will take the amended budget, storyboard and invoice to Mr H. She will explain that they have trimmed the budget as far as it will go without compromising the programme. She will ensure that they understand that this much cannot be taken off an original fair estimate, and it is being done by cutting their margin to practically zero. She will explain the use of Genie College. It was agreed that if the Sales Director agreed the programme she would negotiate staged payments. She would find out whose responsibility it was to choose the girls. She would suggest a Pre production meeting with the Sales Director, Mr H., herself and Simon to discuss the detail of the designer and factory personnel and what the girls would wear.

9. It was agreed that the schedule would be deferred again until confirmation of the programme.

10. Simon agreed to draw up contracts if the programme was confirmed.

11. The only Matters Arising was Elaine wanted to apologize for her expressed anger over the budget and thanked Simon for all his hard work. Simon also apologized for his outburst.

12. There was no other business.

The date of the next meeting would left unconfirmed.

Meeting concluded at 11.05 a.m.

Page 2

Elaine is unhappy about the cut in her salary. Simon has made it clear that for Elaine to agree to a figure £2000 less than his estimate was unwise. Maybe she was a little too eager to do this programme. It certainly has caused a lot of grief so far and they still don't have a guarantee of doing it.

Maybe it is all the pressure of work and the effort that has been put in so far. Meetings can go like this and you should not be despondent if they do, at least they apologized to each other at Item 11!

Simon settles down quietly with a coffee and makes notes before he rings the post production companies.

Has he left anything out? Is there anything else you would like to ask? He still has a voice-over problem because he has yet to book an artist. Some post production companies have good contacts with agencies and will supply a package of artist plus the audio dub. He got the £175 figure from the old production diaries.

You may ask why he is not going to the company he has used before. People do shop around, that way they keep in touch with current prices and facilities. Simon knows what his normal company charges, the prices are on the post production budget. He needs to better them.

Richard at First Post is very helpful, and honest. He is glad to hear that Bob sends his regards and says he has great respect for his

---

Fashions for You. Post Prod. Phone Calls. 11th August 99

1. 925568 - First Post - Ask for Richard (Bob said)
2. 803274 - Edit All - Ask for Tim (Bob said)

Need one day P.P. - Mastered on Beta SP - Need SP Final tape + 4 VHS
Do they do Voice Over
Can they mix in Music, SFX
Computer Generated Graphics
Effects
Some shots are three screen, plus overlaid graphic
Bring Masters, get BITC VHS for off line?
How much?
How much notice do they need?
Will get back this P.M.

camerawork. He has a three-machine SP suite with digital effects, and a graphics generator. He thinks a day and a half is more realistic because, with only a three-machine edit, some of the effects will need to be created and then re-edited. He has a 'library' of voice-over artists he uses, so the audio mixing and dubbing is no problem. He can't see any problems with the effects, he has a sophisticated DVE machine. BITC copies are no problem and, provided there aren't hundreds of masters he will do them at stock cost as it only requires SP to VHS copies. He would like a little time to come up with prices.

This all seems very satisfactory to Simon and he tries Tim, at Edit All. He seems busy and efficient, rather than friendly, explains that he has a mid range non linear system, agrees it would take a day if the tapes are properly logged. He would need the voice-over on DAT but apart from that there are no problems. He doesn't want to get involved with BITC copies, but knows someone who would do them. He wants £900 a day for everything including the edit tapes, an SP master and six VHS copies. Simon will ring him back this afternoon.

It may be that you think all this extra work is unnecessary at this stage. It is costing time and money and there is no promise of the programme. Under normal circumstances you would probably be right. Simon is working to an extremely tight budget. He only has £300 contingency and has already cut the salaries. He is investing the time by trying to protect the money.

Richard rings back. He wants £950 for the whole package, including a voice-over artist from his 'library'. It would be a day and a half, but if it overruns by an hour or so he won't be too bothered. He needs two edit tapes and would charge £20. The BITC copies will be £5 each. He will provide an SP master and charge £10 per VHS copy. Simon thanks him, explains he needs to look at the budget and will ring back.

Now it is your turn! Look back at the post production budget on page 83 and see which you will choose, and why. Richard seems more expensive because extra salaries will be involved, but is he? How much is the difference? Would you go to Tim because non linear sounds 'fun' and anyway 'it is better'? Can we save anything on the budget, or has it gone over again? If we can save anything what do we do? Offer the client a lower figure? Restore the salaries? Go for a bigger contingency? Is this all a bit boring and you will just go on to read the next page? Why? You will have to juggle budgets one day, why not now?

Simon gets out a sheet of paper. Does yours look like his?

Fashions for You. Post Production options. 11 Aug. 99
1. 925568 – First Post – Richard   2. 803274 – Edit All – Tim

Voice Over –			Voice Over –	£ 175
Audio Dub –			Audio Dub –	
Special Effects –			Special Effects –	
On Line –	£ 950		On Line –	£ 900

Total	£ 950	Total	£1075
BITC @ £5 –	£ 50	BITC @ £10 –	£ 100
1/2 Day Director	£ 50		
1/2 Day P.M.	£ 50		
1/2 Day P.A.	£ 20		
4 VHS copies	£ 40		
2 Edit tapes	£ 20		
	----------		----------
	£1180		£1175

Predicted Post Cost

		£15 between
On Line	£ 600	Tim & Richard
Special FX	£ 150	
Voice Over	£ 175	Approx £55
Audio Dub	£ 125	Under budget!!
Stock	£ 180	
	£1230	

Simon is pretty pleased with this hour's work. It has shown that his budget prediction is only about £50 over estimated. He has allowed £30 for duplicating in his indirect cost budget which means that he can take £30 off Richard's duplicating cost. This means Richard is slightly cheaper than Tim, but there is really nothing in it and it would probably go on sandwiches for the second day anyway.

We now have a dilemma. Who do you choose to go to? Why? What happens to the £50 we have saved? Spend it? Give it to the client? It has to be accounted for somewhere.

Simon modifies his post production Budget sheet. He has chosen to go to Richard. Why? Not because he is marginally cheaper on paper, but for two very good reasons. He liked him on the phone, he felt straight away that he could work with him. Video is a team game, the result will always be better, even if it costs a little bit more, if you are working with people you feel happy with. He didn't feel he could get on as well with Tim.

Richard is also providing a 'complete service'. He is sorting out the voice artist, doing the BITC copies and looking after the complete edit. Tim didn't want to get involved in anything other than the edit. Simon didn't check, but he knows that some of these 'mid range' non linear suites are actually off line quality, he would rather preserve SP quality all the way through.

He rings Richard and confirms all the details and prices, and then rings Tim and says that he can't use him this time, but thanks him for his help. Why did he ring Richard first? What would have happened if he rang Tim first, and cancelled him, only to find that Richard had revised some of his prices upwards? A bit embarrassing to have to go back to a supplier, you have just turned down, and say you have changed your mind, don't you think? Elaine is preparing for her meeting tomorrow morning. She, too has a checklist.

Because this is a formal meeting, Elaine is going to type a letter to Mr Hermandes saying 'please find enclosed....' (storyboard and budget) and 'we hope you will look favourably on this quotation for this programme, conceptualized to your specification'. She will mention that their reputation is built on 'on time and on budget', and that he can be assured the quoted figure will not go up and the programme will be delivered in time for the 16th October trade show.

You know about meetings now so we won't sit in on this one. Elaine got on very well with Naomi Findler. It took nearly an hour for Naomi and Mr Hermandes to agree it was exactly what they wanted and to agree

Fashions for You - Meeting Sales Director & Mr H 12th Aug. 99
21 Gothic Rd . - tel. 376281. - 9 a.m.
Sales Director name - Naomi Findler.

<u>Me</u> *Wear Fashions for You shirt! - Clean car.*

<u>Take</u>   *Letter, budget breakdown, storyboard, invoice*
       Notepad, pens, mobile (switch off at Gothic Rd).

<u>Explain</u> *Simon has cut budget as far as it will go. We have*
made sacrifices over our margins because we want
to do programme.
          It will stay as storyboard and be delivered on time.

<u>If pushed</u> *We could drop another £50 because of the deal we*
have done with Post, but no more

<u>Negotiate</u> *Staged payments. 20% now, another 40% at end of*
production, last 40% on delivery? prompt payment?

Smile a lot! Look confident! Say please and thank you!

the price. Naomi said she realized the problems of balancing budgets, it was something she did every day. She offered to build in a small contingency by saying 'please stick to the figure quoted, but if you do overspend you can go up to £8500 without further reference to me'.

She agreed that if the staged payments were sent to Mr Hermandes, and he approved them as the work had been done, she would pass them to accounts for a seven-day payment. She would not, however, be moved off 25% on signature of contract, 25% at the end of production and the remainder on completion. She gave Elaine back the invoice for the £250 because it would be simpler just to invoice for 25%. She looks forward to working with Ace Productions and will leave Mr Hermandes to make the necessary arrangements.

We've got the programme! This book has to go on to production and post production paperwork, and you will have to go on filling in your production file! Fun isn't it!

Schedules and deadlines

We have said that schedules and budgets go hand in hand. This is because if you decide that this will be a two-day shoot, then the budget will show the cost of that two days. This is why Simon had to change the post production budget when he decided that the on line edit would become 1½ days.

If you overestimate the schedule then the budget will be higher than necessary, possibly losing you the programme. The reverse is worse. If Simon had merely accepted Richard's figure without costing in the other half day for director, production manager and PA, who would have paid them? It certainly couldn't have come out of the budget.

The thing you will notice about this section's heading is that I have put schedules and deadlines together. They also go hand in hand. The elements that make up the programme must be scheduled to happen on a particular day. Everything that is needed for that day must be done by then. For instance if we are shooting at the college on Friday the staging and catwalk must be finished by Thursday night.

Schedules also go with contracts. We have to arrange for the crew to be there to shoot the catwalk scenes on Friday. This may all seem very logical, but it only wants one mistake or forgotten prop, for instance, to throw the whole schedule out resulting in re-negotiating contracts and yet more money. I have never yet known of a crew who turned up to be told 'sorry we don't need you until tomorrow' and gone away happy, not wanting paying for today! If you are talking £500 a day for crew, that is a lot of money to come out of a £300 contingency, particularly as you are over budget already.

One deadline that cannot be moved is the completion date. However I would suggest that you leave as much of a cushion as possible. Clients do sometimes want a last minute change, for which they will pay a late

PRODUCTION SCHEDULE

Fashions for You.   Completion 8th Oct. 99

Task	Dates	Contract issued	Who Does?
Hand over	8th Oct. 99		Simon & Elaine
On Line	5th & 6th Oct. 99		Simon & Elaine
**Voice over	5th Oct. 99 9 A.M.		Simon & Elaine
Client viewing	30th Sept. 99		Simon & Elaine
Off Line	27th & 28th Sept. 99		Simon, Elaine, P.A.
BITC copies	24th Sept. 99		Simon
Shoot College	22nd Sept. 99		Simon, Elaine, P.A.
Shoot Factory	21st Sept. 99 p.m.		Simon, Elaine, P.A.
Shoot Design	21st Sept. 99 a.m.		Simon, Elaine, P.A.
**Rehearse Girls	20th Sept. 99		Simon & Elaine
Complete staging	17th Sept. 99		Elaine
Logs	16th Sept. 99		Elaine & P.A.
Camera Cards	16th Sept. 99		Elaine & P.A.
Clothes from F f Y	16th Sept. 99		P.A.
Banner (Graphics)	15th Sept. 99		P.A.
Organize Catering	15th Sept. 99		P.A.
Prod Meeting	13th Sept. 99		Simon, Elaine, P.A.
Call sheets	13th Sept. 99		Elaine & P.A.
Music Delivered	8th Sept. 99		Simon

Notes.
P.A. required 13th, 15th, 16th, 21st, 22nd, 27th, 28th Sept., and 5th Oct.
only (for on line)
Elaine to book.

Staging/Catwalk must be in place by 17th Sept.

Phone Sally (college) to see about audition and rehearsing the girls.

Check with Richard when we are doing V/O.

change fee. This programme has to make a trade fair on 16th October. I would suggest that the programme is handed to the client on the 8th.

The client will be reassured that 'on budget and on time', means that you appreciate they have deadlines too, and are more likely to use you again if it has been a relaxing experience for them. Beware, though, the client who sets near impossible deadlines, only to tell you that they moved their deadline forward to cover any eventualities.

It is always best to work up some trust between both of you. Ask when the absolute deadline is and reassure them they will have it a week or two before that.

Simon is working on his schedule.

This is Ace Productions' schedule. Yours may be different, but the principle will be the same. Simon knows they have got the programme because Elaine phoned to tell him, but nothing is ever promised until it is in writing. It is Thursday. He will now double check the budget so he is totally familiar with it, check the production diary and make sure everything is up to date, particularly the petty cash sheets and receipts.

Nothing else will happen until he sees the contract from Fashions for You. He has scheduled the hard work to start on 13th September, but there is much to be done before that. You will see that he has left dates out of the schedule. Some are weekends, some are catch up days, some are just in case anything goes wrong days. It may look a bit unnecessary, but he knows if something can go wrong, it will.

Contracts

A contract is defined as an enforceable agreement between two or more parties. It may be verbal, but that can be difficult to prove in a court of law, or written. Because it is an agreement between parties, often both (or all) parties sign it with a witness present to agree the signatures.

Some contracts run into pages and are full of legal jargon. Some are more simple and just say 'you agree to do this and I agree to do that'. The IVCA have produced a draft agreement that can be used as a guide. Ace Productions is only involved in small scale productions and has drawn up a couple of simple forms with help from their lawyer.

Unless you are directly employing union staff, or planning a very long (feature length!) programme, you would be best to keep it simple and understandable.

It is Thursday 19th August. Elaine opens her mail.

FASHIONS FOR YOU
exciting, affordable clothing for you

21, Gothic Road
Genie Town
GT64 2TX

Telephone: 96795 376281   *Fax: 96795 397401*

Ace Productions
39 West Street
Genie Town GT64 6DE

17th August 1999

Dear Elaine Booker,

The Sales Director and I would like to thank you for coming to see us on Thursday last.

We appreciate the effort you have put in on our behalf to date and would confirm that we would like to offer you the production of our programme for an agreed figure of £8215.

Enclosed are two copies of the contract. Please sign one copy and return it to me. The other copy should also be signed and retained for your records.

If you wish to submit an invoice for £2053.75p, to represent the agreed 25% of the total figure, I will ensure that it is passed for payment.

If it can be arranged, we would like the opportunity of selecting the girls to be used. We will then arrange the clothes we would like them to wear.

Please keep me informed of the stages the programme is going through, and do not hesitate to contact me if I can be of help.

Best Wishes,

Yours sincerely,

Pat Hermandes

Pat Hermandes

Projects Officer

FASHIONS FOR YOU
exciting, affordable clothing for you

SUPPLIER CONTRACT

This agreement is made on 16th August 1999 Between

1.   **Fashions for You**, 21 Gothic Road, Genie Town. GT64 2TX

and

2.   **Ace Productions**, 39 West Street, Genie Town. GT64 6DE

It is hereby agreed that:

Ace Productions will supply a video programme following the approved treatment, storyboard and script for the agreed sum of **£8215** (eight thousand two hundred and fifteen pounds).

The delivery day will be no later than the 14th day of October 1999.

The format of the supplied tape will be VHS.

The supplier will produce, if requested, proof of Public Liability Insurance for no less than £3,000,000 (three million pounds).

The supplier warrants that at all times they, or their contractors, are on our premises they will abide by any Health and Safety at Work regulations that are in force.

Fashions for You will provide the clothing necessary for the fashion sequences.

Fashions for You will provide access to its Design Office and Factory on dates to be notified by the supplier.

Fahions for You will arrange staged payments as follows:

25% of the final invoice on the return of this contract.

25% of the final invoice on the approved completion of shooting.

50% of the final invoice on the final acceptance of the programme.

These payments will be made within seven days of the approval of the invoice.

Signed by   **Print Name**

Duly authorized for and on behalf of the producer

Signed by *Pat Hermandes*   **Print Name**   Mr Pat Hermandes

Duly authorized for and on behalf of the client

Elaine studies these documents twice, and it would pay you to do the same. The first is a formal letter asking for the contracts to be signed and requesting the first invoice. It also includes a request that they should select the girls. This should not be ignored. There have been court battles over non payment by a client because of something that was said in a letter. It is possible that it could be read as a contract. They asked, you ignored it, they didn't like the girls and withheld the final payment.

It also contains a reference to 'keep me informed'. This would be natural good manners anyway, but is also a form of insurance policy for you. If the client agrees each stage there can be no argument later. Be aware, though, that some clients (particularly project officers!) can become a real nuisance. They want to get out of the office and see how video programmes are made. Before you know where you are they fancy themselves as directors and try to take over, resulting in frustration and loss of time (time is money!). You need to be firm from the outset.

The contract is a straightforward simple affair. It details what you must do and what they agree to do. Note the reference to public liability insurance. We will cover this later but, for now, it is something you must have. Notice too that they are requiring you to abide by their health and safety policy. If you are at all unsure of what that involves, ask to see a copy. All companies are required by law to draw up such a policy.

Now Simon needs to draw up some contracts for the people he will employ. We will look at two different types, rather than watch him fill them all in. The basic format is the same and you may want to make up your own. What must go in is exactly what you want done and exactly what you are offering in return. They must be signed and dated. You must send two copies. One for you, one for them. Never shoot anything until the contract has been signed.

This is the contributor release form that Simon uses for people who 'contribute' to the programme. The girls, designers and factory staff will get a similar form. It is basically designed to say 'I will contribute to your programme (as a musician, model, designer, factory worker) for this amount of money on (or by) this date.

This form must be signed before any shooting takes place. The girls and staff will have to be contacted, before the crew turn up, and agree to appear by signing the form. It is no good turning up and then people say they have had second thoughts. Provided you have a signed agreement absences will be covered under insurance (more later). No signature – you lose money!

Ace Productions
Video Programmes on Budget & on Time

39, West Street
Genie Town
GT64 6DE

Tel: 96795 230871
Fax: 96795 230858

23rd August 1999

CONTRIBUTOR RELEASE FORM

PROGRAMME TITLE: Fashions for You Video presenter

CONTRIBUTION: Background Music track

CONTRIBUTOR NAME: Julian Wisher

CONTRIBUTOR ADDRESS: 79, Parkside. Wistholme. GT64 6AX

Ace Productions agree to pay £200 (two hundred pounds) for the composition of an original piece of music reflecting the vibrancy of youth which must stay within the style and content of the sample tape previously submitted.

The piece is to be five minutes in length with cutting points at thirty seconds, one minute and two minutes.

The final tape is to be supplied, properly labelled and indexed on DAT, with a cassette copy, no later than the 8th September 1999.

All rights to this piece will be retained by us and its use is to be restricted exclusively to the above programme.

By signing this agreement you agree that:

1) Failure to produce the piece by the deadline date stated, will result in this agreement being cancelled.

2) You pass all copyright in the work to the company.

3) You waive your moral rights under section 77 and section 80 of the Copyright Design and Patents Act of 1988.

Signed by the Contributor   Date

Signed by the Producer *Elaine Booker*   Date 23rd August 1999

Elaine Booker

Producer

There are three interesting things in this form. Even when the form has been signed the contract has a time limit. If the music is not produced by the 8th September the contract expires. Julian gets no money and it leaves time for Simon to go to someone else, there is nothing Julian can do about it no matter how much time he has spent on the project.

Julian is passing all copyright to Ace Productions. That means he no longer owns this piece of music. Some music commissioned as background for adverts has done really well. It is the company, not the musician that gets the royalties! Often musicians will want extra money to sign the rights away.

There is a reference to the Copyright Design and Patents Act. Under this Act the 'Moral Rights' of a contributor have to be acknowledged, by way of a credit. Ace Productions have enough trouble with Julian without giving him a credit! If this clause is not put in, you could find the credits last longer than the programme.

Simon is now going to do a contract for Richard.

This form is the one that Simon uses for his suppliers. Richard at First Post, Bob for the crew, and the college. The form is essentially an order form, but the lawyer has made it into a legally binding contract by suggesting the heading at the top, and an acknowledgement of agreement by signature at the bottom. Again this would be used in the event of an insurance claim.

It is important to understand the difference in these forms. The college will get an 'order' to supply the services, but not the girls. They are being employed directly by Ace Productions and will get the same form that Julian got.

It may be that your course expects you to design a contract form. You can put anything in it you like, provided it is fair and reasonable. The one rule is that it must be simple, understandable and cover everything you want. It would be no good, for instance, agreeing an SP crew with Bob on the phone, not specifying it on the contract and then moaning when a VHS crew turned up because that was all he had on the day.

Some people may tell you that they trust their suppliers and there is really no need to get them a contract. Try telling me that when you turn up for a shoot miles from home with four very expensive actors, only to find no crew because they forgot to put it in their diary! Never leave anything to chance. The pre production side of the programme will take the longest to do because it has to ensure that nothing is left out or left

Ace Productions
Video Programmes on Budget & on Time

39, West Street
Genie Town
GT64 6DE
Tel: 96795 230871
Fax: 96795 230858

SUPPLIER ORDER
23rd August 1999

To: First Post
     Unit 12, South Business Park
     Genie Town GT64 19TQ

THIS ORDER WILL FORM A CONTRACT WHEN SIGNED AND RETURNED.

Please supply:

10 Beta SP to BITC VHS tapes from our masters	50.00
on **24th September 1999**	
2 SP Edit tapes	20.00
1½ Days On Line Edit (3 M/c SP) to include supplying and	950.00
recording a voice-over artist of our choice, all special effects,	
graphics, audio dub and mix of SFX, V/O and our supplied	
music, on one Master SP tape.	
Work to be carried out on the **5th and 6th October 1999.**	
4 VHS copies from the above master	40.00

TOTAL   £1060.00

Notes:
A.   Voice-over to be selected from your tape samples
B.   Music will be supplied on DAT
C.   Edit Log will be in the form of Time Code In/Out points

If you are in agreement with the above please sign, date and return one copy

Signed on behalf of First Post   Date

Signed on behalf of Ace Productions   *Elaine Booker*   Date
Elaine Booker. Producer   23rd August 1999

to chance. That way the creative side of making the programme can go smoothly, on time and on budget.

Elaine, as producer and director, will ring the college and arrange for Mr Hermandes to meet the girls so that he can choose which he wants to use. She will also arrange to go to First Post and listen to the voice-over tapes. She will select two or three and take them to Mr Hermandes for the final choice.

Copyright

This 'basics' level of book is not intended to go into all the legal ramifications of copyright law. What we can do is to take a simplified look at the concept and its meaning to you. If you want to go into more depth there are excellent books on the subject or you could buy *The Copyright, Design and Patents Act of 1988*, which applies to the UK, the principles of which are incorporated in similar laws around the world. Copyright goes hand in hand with 'permissions', which we will look at next.

The basics are that everything belongs to someone. This may be complicated by more than one person owning parts of one thing. A song is a good example, the writer owns the words, the singer the lyrics, the performers their performance, the record company the recording. This is why to simplify things a record company may employ these people and contract them to relinquish all rights (as Ace Productions have with Julian). Depending on how famous the people involved are this may involve lots of money or a refusal to give up their rights.

Someone owns the streets, in London the Metropolitan Police have strict rules about what you can and cannot shoot in them. Another example is the London Underground who make a charge, based on what the video will be used for, to shoot on their premises.

There is nothing that you can use without permission from the owner. It does not work to say you own a famous artist's CD, because you bought it, and therefore you can do what you like with it. The Mechanical Copyright Protection Society (in the UK, but international agreements exist), protect the owners of the recording. You are breaking the law if you copy your CD onto cassette to play in the car, and you certainly can't make a copy for a friend! For similar reasons you cannot play it in public. The Performing Rights Society protects the public performance of works.

They will require details of what you are going to do and then arrange a licence for you to do it.

The law has been interpreted in the courts to mean that you own yourself. A case has shown that a member of the public, who was photographed by a newspaper against their wishes, had the right to give, or refuse, permission for the photograph to be taken. Famous people are usually not covered, but there are cases in law where even this has been challenged.

If you want to make sure your contract is watertight you should make reference to copyright somewhere. In Julian's contract he signed away his rights to the ownership of the music, and his moral rights to be credited. Ace Productions effectively bought the copyright.

The alternatives to contracting a musician to compose a piece of music specially is to buy 'copyright free' music (but even this has restrictions placed on its use), or use 'music library' compositions which are free to use, but a transfer fee is levied by MCPS. The cost is dependent on the use. Examples of year 2000 costs would be £25 per 30 seconds of use for Simon's corporate video. It was by looking at the MCPS rate card that Simon worked out that five minutes of library music would cost him £250, therefore he needed to offer Julian less! The same piece of library music would cost £993 per 30 secs if used on a commercial (ITV) advert across the whole broadcast region. There is additionally a small (£8) fee for the issue of the licence.

Permissions

Permissions and copyright are both the subject of various laws. The simple difference is that works of art, photographs and music (for example), belong to the author of that work and you have to pay that person to use it. That is copyright law. Equally buildings, parks, buses, underground trains and the like also belong to some organization. This organization has a right, but not a duty, to charge you to feature it in your video. This means that you need the owner's permission before you can shoot anything anywhere, unless you own it and give yourself permission! The only exception to this is that it is generally accepted that tourists will video the 'sights' for their own personal use. This isn't always the case and there may be notices posted to say 'no photographs or filming'.

The two examples of permissions we have in the Fashions for You programme are the Fashions for You premises, and the college. Fashions for You have given (free) permission because it is in their interest to do so. They have put parameters around their permission in their contract where they say 'on dates to be notified' and 'comply with our Health and Safety policy'. You would not have permission if you go on any other date or do not comply with their wishes. The college has charged a fee for 'the use of their facilities'. They have given permission, but reserved their right to charge. They would not charge their students to make videos on their premises for course work, but might if it was for public broadcast.

Sometimes permissions can be negotiated at a nil or reduced fee. Colleges often arrange with shopping malls or parks for permission for their students to shoot their course work programmes on these premises.

Never assume you can shoot anywhere. At best you will have the video-tape confiscated, at worst you will end up in court. Always get permission in writing (you need it for the production diary, anyway!) and take it with you. You will never get away with 'the person at head office said it was OK', or 'my teacher said do it quickly while no one is looking'!

Insurance

Some insurance is required by law (e.g. your car), some is a sensible precaution (e.g. travel insurance). By law you must have liability insurance if you are a company. This covers accidents to your employees. It is sensible to check that they are covered if they are working for you on location, as opposed to your place of work; it is not automatic. You may combine this insurance with public liability insurance (which is voluntary). You would be stupid not to have public liability because if people do fall over, or have accidents, on your premises the certainty is that they will say 'I'll sue' before you can say 'I'm sorry, can I get you a bandage'.

You will notice that Fashions for You require Ace Productions (in the contract) to be covered for at least £3,000,000.

Beyond these two insurances, you can insure anything else you want to. How much you pay depends on how much risk the insurance company thinks is involved. Famous stars insure the parts of their body that they are famous for (legs, face, voice etc.). It may be that you need to shoot a scene on a sunny day in the park. You have budgeted crew and cast for two days but can't afford to wait three. Someone will insure you for the loss of money if it rains. How much is dependent on how much risk they think is involved and how much money you want covered. It would obviously cost less in the summer than the winter.

Simon uses the same company each time, they are specialists in video cover, and he insures against cancellation of the shoot, due to crew or performers not turning up or any unforeseen reason (the building burnt down last night!), the loss or destruction of any master or edit tape (up to the cost of a reshoot or redit). He also insures against being let down by a supplier (the edit suite is out of action). This is a special type of insurance because he should sue the supplier, but he has an arrangement with his company that they pay him and they sue the supplier, probably for a lot more than they paid Simon.

The insurance company charge him (as you saw from the budget) £250 per shoot. Larger companies doing more videos per year than Ace Productions would get an annual quote, which would work out cheaper than paying £250 for each production.

You would be advised to think about what you want to insure for your productions; £250 seems a small price to pay if you lost the one-day shoot at the college. Crew, performers, staging, facilities etc. comes to over £1000 and there is only £300 in contingency. £700 is an awful lot of pocket money for you to lose.

Before we finally get to the end of the pre production stage there are some loose ends remaining. One is to get the production diary up to date and do the first invoice to be sent with the signed contract.

Elaine has to set a date for the last pre production meeting with the client, to discuss the schedule and the audition for the girls.

While he waits for the Ace Productions contracts to come back and for Elaine to arrange the audition and meeting, Simon will do the first invoice.

Simon will also do the 'Actual' column of the pre production budget to see whether he is over or under at this stage.

You can see that, because all the receipts have been filed in the right places and all the time sheets have been filled in, it has been easy for Simon to extract the information he needs. Elaine actually took longer over the script than she had thought. They spent less on food and petrol, but more on mail and telephone. They have decided not to use the PA until the production and post production stage so have saved her salary.

Ace Productions
Video Programmes on Budget & on Time

39, West Street
Genie Town
GT64 6DE
Tel: 96795 230871
Fax: 96795 230858

INVOICE

Fashions for You	Invoice Number: 109835
21 Gothic Road	Invoice Date: 23rd August 1999
Genie Town GT64 2TX	Account No: F005

DESCRIPTION	AMOUNT £
Agreed 25% of final invoice on signature and return of contract	2053.75

Client Name: Mr Hermandes

Cheques should be made payable to: Ace Productions

Cheques should be sent to: The Production Manager
Ace Productions, 39 West Street, Genie Town,
GT64 6DE

They have come out £77 under budget, which makes this a very good budget estimate.

You will have appreciated by now that the majority of the work that has happened so far has been in getting and developing the programme, and then, by leaving nothing out, ensuring that we have a smooth shoot and edit.

Ace Productions. – Budget – (Estimated v. Actual) – Client Mr Pat Hermandes.

FASHIONS for YOU – VIDEO PRESENTER. BUDGET

BUDGET BREAKDOWN FOR PRE PRODUCTION

ITEM		DAYS	RATE	ESTIMATE	ACTUAL	DIFF
Research		0.5	£80.00	£40.00	£40.00	
Script		0.25	£80.00	£20.00	£40.00	+£20
Storyboard		0.5	£80.00	£40.00	£40.00	
Budget		0.5	£80.00	£40.00	£40.00	
Transport			£60.00	£60.00	£45.00	–£15
Subsistence			£125.00	£125.00	£118.00	–£07
Telephone/Mail			£35.00	£35.00	£40.00	+£05
Location recce		1.5	£100.00	£150.00	£150.00	
Production Manager	*modified*	10	£80.00	£800.00	£800.00	
Director	*modified*	10	£80.00	£800.00	£800.00	
P.A.	*Now prod & post*	2	£40.00	£80.00	£0.00	–£80
	Sub Totals £			£2190.00	£2113.00	–£77

page 2

Production

You will see the importance of the pre production stage from the amount of time we have spent in the planning and preparation for our production.

Production is the actual shooting of the programme, in this case at three locations over two days. As you will see from the budget this is the most expensive stage of the whole process; these two days will cost more than the ten days of pre production.

In order that this stage goes according to plan, and schedule, we still have some paperwork that is concerned with the shooting itself. Nothing must be left to chance; we could lose a large amount of money if anything is allowed to go wrong. Short of major catastrophes, which will be covered by insurance, anything that does go wrong will be due to your lack of paperwork and entirely your fault.

Ace Productions has a problem that is typical of small companies struggling to make a name for themselves and survive in this difficult, and cutthroat, business. If you look back at the final budget sheets you will see that they only charged for ten days of pre production; yet the pre production stage lasted from the arrival of a request by letter on July 8th until now, September 3rd. If they had charged Fashions for You the cost of the whole duration they would have been so far over the client's budget that they would not have got the programme.

The assumption must be that they were working on other programmes during these three months or doing their part time jobs. Realistically there were many days when nothing happened at all and then a few when everything happened, including a late Friday night and a Saturday!

The same is going to happen with the Production stage. There are only two salaried days allocated on September 21st and 22nd, nearly three weeks away, but there is much to do before that.

Production meetings

The thinking behind a production meeting is to ensure that everything that needs to be dealt with is allocated to a named person, and everybody knows what is happening, and when. Nothing can now be left to chance.

This first production meeting will close the pre production phase and prepare for the production stage. Some people will say that this is actually the last pre production meeting. You may see it this way and want to file it under 'Pre production'. I will not argue with that because whatever is easiest, and feels right to you, is what you do. Simon and Elaine like to make it the first production meeting, because it is wholly concerned with the two days' shoot, and they will put the agenda and minutes in the production diary under the 'Meetings' section of the 'Production' element.

Fashions for You

Production Meeting   6th September 1999   9 a.m.   Elaine & Simon

AGENDA

1. Update on Contracts.
2. Update on Meeting with Mr H.
3. Update on Meeting with College.
4. Update on employment of P.A.
5. Discuss Schedule (attached) and cover all items.
6. Matters Arising.
7. A.O.B.

Meeting expected to last 2 hours.

You will have seen throughout this book that although there are only two people involved in this company and they work together and see each other all the time, there are times when they will chat about something and times when they formally call a meeting. This is professionalism. It is very difficult to put accounts of the occasional 'corridor chats' in the diary. If it is important – call a meeting!

Have a look at Elaine's agenda and see if you thought of all the items she wants covered. Perhaps more importantly think whether she has left anything out that you will have to bring it up under AOB.

You will see that the 'loose ends' are being tied up. Rather than sit in on the meeting, we will look at the minutes.

Confidentiality clauses

You can see that nothing is ever simple! Just when you thought that everything was covered and running along happily this happens. Simon now has to sort out the confidentiality problem and look at the PA schedule in terms of hours. He also has to revise the budget.

Confidentiality is a big issue with companies. To take Fashions for You as an example, they spend months working on designs, colours, ranges and so forth in order to make their product competitive and unique. If their competitors find out what they are doing there is a very real chance that they will produce a near identical range less expensively.

Because it is written into their contract of employment, all the employees are sworn to secrecy. A casual 'we've got a lovely shirt in smoke blue for next season' could mean instant dismissal. The chances of working again in this industry sector will be slim because prospective employers will be told.

Because it is in the contract the employee has committed a breach of contract, which may be considered serious enough for it to result in court action to recover large sums of money in compensation.

It is understood that production companies will abide by the rules of confidentiality, because they need to work and earn money. You won't get far if you go and tell a rival company what you are working on. It saves a lot of trouble to say 'we have done similar programmes' than run through your client list with a prospective client. Sometimes a client will write a confidentiality clause into your contract. This is one method of ensuring you don't break the rules. Generally there is an accepted mutual trust between client and producer.

What has happened here is that Naomi has realized that Ace Productions are not employing people as staff, but as contractors. This means that to ensure secrecy everyone involved must sign to say that they will not give away any details of the Fashions for You range. It may only be a month before the official launch of next season's range, but that is long enough for a competitor to counter it with something of his or her own.

Simon has now got to check the wording with the lawyer and then incorporate in the contributor release forms for the girls, and construct a simple 'Confidentiality Statement' for the crew, editing personnel, voice-over and audience to sign. Confidentiality is well understood in any business and there should be no problem with the shooting or editing crew signing the form on the day, it is a risk but so minimal that it isn't worth considering. If the audience don't want to sign they don't watch; it is that simple!

Some companies are extremely sensitive about this issue. There have been cases where producers have to give an undertaking that they are not working for a rival company. There have also been cases where production companies have negotiated a 'retainer fee', whereby they agree to work exclusively for a particular company in a sector and turn down work from others.

Simon has rung the lawyer and they have come up with an agreed clause: 'I hereby warrant that I will not pass on any details of the content of this programme to a third party, and will disclose any conflicting interest I may have with a similar company. By signing this contract I understand that I am legally bound to respect the need for confidentiality'.

The confidentiality clause statement will be sent as a separate form with the contracts for the girls and he has also been advised to ensure that anybody involved with the programme, including himself and Elaine, must also sign them.

The lawyer advised Simon to have these photocopied and sent to Naomi for her to keep on file. The reason behind this is that the lawyer feels that if there is a breach of confidentiality the task of tracing its source will be so enormous that Ace Productions really don't want to get involved in it.

Nobody is going to admit that they were responsible. It could be any of the Fashions for You work force, anyone at the college or any member of the crew. If there is a leak it is better that Fashions for You sort it out themselves.

Fashions for You

Production Meeting   6th September 1999   9 a.m.   Elaine & Simon

MINUTES

1. Elaine has received contracts back from Julian, Bob, Richard and the College. There were no problems with any of them.
2. Elaine met with Mr H. on September 1st (notes in Prod Diary). The date set for the Design and Factory shoot was confirmed as 21st Sept. Four people in both Design and Factory have been selected, representing a true cross section of their workforce. Names and addresses are in the Prod Diary. An area will be set aside as Simon requested at both locations with space around them. Mr H. is ensuring that the clothes the girls will wear will be the same as the designs and manufacture. This will be confirmed in writing when Naomi has selected them. A problem has arisen with the clothes that were to have been given to the girls. Naomi had overlooked the fact that they will be wearing next season's clothes for the catwalk sequence and she wants a confidentiality clause put into their contract. She also requires anyone involved in the shooting, editing or watching of this sequence to sign confidentiality statements. She will ensure that the girls receive some of this season's clothes as a token of F for Y's appreciation.
3. Mr H. and Naomi came to the college on 2nd Sept. and met Sally Beagle. They have selected four girls (names and addresses in Prod Diary) representing a cross section of their sales target audience. Elaine pointed out to them that the agreement was three girls and that was all that was budgeted for. Naomi offered a further £100 to cover the cost of the fourth girl and any other work that may be needed. This will also be put in writing. Sally showed us the stage and catwalk plan (photocopy in Prod Diary) and assured us that it would be completed by 17th Sept. She will now rehearse all the girls in the group as an exercise and has agreed to us coming in on the 20th Sept. at 6 p.m. to see how they are performing.

   Simon will see the lawyer about the confidentiality clauses and add the £100 to the budget. He will now arrange contracts for the Design, Factory and College participants.
4. Elaine has contacted the Agency they use for a P.A. One of the girls they have used before has been contracted for the eight dates Simon suggested. The Agency now does not agree day rates and will charge £5 an hour. They will send confirmation when we agree the times required. Simon will work on this because it may now be possible to have her for more days but less hours each day. He will produce a revised schedule for the Agency by tonight.
5. The schedule was discussed and it was agreed that this agenda item would be carried forward to the meeting of 13th Sept. when the P.A. will be present.
6. There were no Matters Arising, or Other Business.

The meeting concluded at 10.50 a.m.

Simon has now decided that, in view of the extra work involved he will ask for the PA for six hours on the 9th, 13th and 15th of Sept. and then eight hours on both shooting days, both off line and both on line days. This is a total of 66 hours at £5 per hour, totalling £330. The budget allowed for eight days at £40 (£320) and the extra £10 will come from the extra £100 Naomi has promised.

Simon discusses this with Elaine who will contact the agency to get agreement before Simon raises an order to put this in order formally.

Second production meeting

The PA has been confirmed and Elaine calls a production meeting for 9 a.m. on the 9th of September. Why did she pick this date and time, when the schedule said the 13th Sept.? You will notice the agenda isn't in this book, what would you put in it? If you had called this meeting who would be present?

You will have to organize and run your production meetings so why don't you draw up an agenda, have the meeting and then see what happened at Ace Productions' meeting. The way to learn is to try to think of everything and then compare it with reality. That way if you make mistakes they won't cost you anything because you will be able to 'put it down to experience'.

You will also notice that I haven't included the minutes. You know what minutes look like now and anyway you had the meeting and didn't send me a copy of your minutes! Did you draw up the minutes and circulate them to all those present?

That leaves me with the task of explaining what happened at Ace Productions' meeting so that you can compare it with your own.

The new PA was greeted (was she at your meeting?), this is her first morning and she needs to know what she has to do. Her name is Poppy. People will happily sit around doing nothing all day, if they are being paid for it, so her schedule needs to be sorted out.

Julian's music arrived this morning (as promised) together with an invoice. The Fashions for You cheque arrived yesterday. The contracts need sorting out for the girls and the Fashions for You staff. The confidentiality clauses need to be drawn up for Simon, Elaine, Poppy and all the crew. The catering has to be organized. The banner, with the Fashions for You logo, has to be collected. Call sheets, camera cards and logs need doing. The clothes have to be collected. Poppy is going to have a busy Thursday and Monday!

Simon handed out the revised schedule (opposite). Does it look like

PRODUCTION SCHEDULE

Fashions for You.

Completion 8th Oct. 99

Task	Dates	Contract issued	Who Does?
Hand over	8th Oct. 99		Simon & Elaine
On Line	5th & 6th Oct. 99	*Yes*	Simon & Elaine, PA
**Voice over	5th Oct. 99. *9 A.M.*		Simon & Elaine, PA
Client viewing	30th Sept. 99		Simon & Elaine
Off Line	27th & 28th Sept. 99		Simon, Elaine, P.A.
BITC copies	24th Sept. 99		Simon
Shoot College	22nd Sept. 99	*Yes*	Simon, Elaine, P.A.
Shoot Factory	21st Sept. 99 p.m.	*Yes*	Simon, Elaine, P.A.
Shoot Design	21st Sept. 99 a.m.	*Yes*	Simon, Elaine, P.A.
**Rehearse Girls	20th Sept. 99	*6 p.m.*	Simon & Elaine
Complete staging	17th Sept. 99	*Agreed*	Elaine
Logs	~~16th Sept. 99~~ *15th*		Elaine & P.A.
Camera Cards	~~16th Sept. 99~~ *15th*		Elaine & P.A.
Clothes from F f Y	~~16th Sept. 99~~ *13th*		P.A.
Banner (Graphics)	~~15th Sept. 99~~ *13th*		P.A.
Organize Catering	~~15th Sept. 99~~ *13th*		P.A.
Prod Meeting	~~13th Sept. 99~~ *9th*		Simon, Elaine, P.A.
Call sheets	~~13th Sept. 99~~ *15th*		Elaine & P.A.
Music Delivered	8th Sept. 99	*Yes (9th)*	Simon

Notes

PA required 13th, 15th, ~~16th,~~ 21st, 22nd, 27th, 28th Sept. and 5th Oct. only (for on line) *now 9th, 13th, 15th, (6 hrs). 21st, 22nd, 27th, 28th, 5th, 6th (8hrs)*

Staging/catwalk must be in place by 17th Sept. *(agreed)*

Phone Sally (college) to see about audition and rehearsing the girls ✓

Check with Richard when we are doing V/O. *a.m. 5th – Which artist?*

Elaine to listen to V/O library 10th Sept.

yours, or didn't you revise it? The programme grows and changes as it goes along. If all this is documented in the production diary you will be able to keep track of it. There is no 'it will be all right on the night' at Ace Productions.

Working with a PA

Employing staff, albeit on a part time basis, is a big step for any company. You will remember that, under the health and safety regulations, you have a duty of care with regard to staff welfare. This will include things that you may not have thought of. It is all very well for you to sit in a freezing office with your coat on, but regulations govern the temperature of offices that employees can be expected to work in. Have you got a smoking or non-smoking policy? Employees are entitled to breaks; the intervals between each and the duration of those breaks is laid down. You can sit on the floor and play with your computer; employees can't, and there are regulations for that too! All this is covered by the fact that employees must be given a safe, healthy, working environment.

Laws are in force regarding what you can expect from your staff and what they can expect from you. Human rights legislation is big business. Everything is covered from abuse to harassment.

You will need delegation and diplomacy skills. Many a misunderstanding has blown into a major confrontation. Major companies have problems because the boss won't let the staff do anything without being told how to do it first, or checked up on while they are doing it. If you employ someone then you have to trust him or her to do a job without constant interference from you. They may do it differently to you, but does that matter if it is done efficiently and effectively?

Throughout this book I have tried to give you an insight into running a business. There is a world of difference between doing your final project, together with some sort of production diary, on a video course and actually running a successful video production company.

You can see that it hasn't been easy for Ace Productions. All of reality is here and you could do a lot worse than identify with them and then see if you want to be part of the business (doing camerawork, for example), or actually have the worry of running a business.

Elaine has agreed to bring Poppy up to speed with the programme and run through the production diary with her. They all agree that her first job after that is to organize the sandwiches and make the coffee for lunch!

Simon has made out a confidentiality clause statement and modified the contributor release forms. They are on the computer so Poppy is going to print a statement form for Elaine, Simon and herself and then get the girls' names out of the production diary and send them each a contract.

She will take the Fashions for You cheque and copy some details onto the first invoice. What details? Why? Not until then will she pay it into the bank. When Simon and Elaine have listened to Julian's music, and approved it, she will be given a cheque for Julian and she will copy some details from it onto Julian's invoice before posting it. In which section of the production file will she file his invoice?

The answers to these questions are to do with how a business is run. The Fashions for You cheque is payment for an Ace Productions' invoice. The invoice is correctly filed in 'Invoices'. Now it has been paid it needs to have written onto it the date it was paid and the cheque number. Ace Productions also write the paying-in slip number on the invoice. Banks do lose cheques and in a busy production schedule it is easier to go to the production diary for all the information than to sift through paying-in stubs.

What about Julian's invoice? You didn't say file it under 'invoices' did you? There is a subtle difference here. It is his invoice, but your receipt. You paid out money that will be accounted for on the budget sheet and will be offset against tax. Poppy will file it with all the other receipts in the 'Receipts' section. First she will write on it the date it was paid and the cheque number. If Julian claims he hasn't been paid (post does get lost), she will know where to find the information she needs to cancel the cheque. It is all in the production diary.

Poppy has been employed to do these things. Elaine and Simon are busy with other things. Poppy has been given responsibility. This is making good use of her employment. Elaine may discreetly have a look to see if these two documents have been filed correctly, but if she is going to sit on top of Poppy and tell her how to do things why is she employing her?

Before she goes home until Monday Poppy sorts out the confidentiality clause statements and the contracts for the girls.

You will see that the confidentiality clause statement is very simple. It would stand up in law, if the need arose, and includes a 'conflicting interest' clause. This is there to give the person signing it the chance

Ace Productions
Video Programmes on Budget & on Time

39, West Street
Genie Town
GT64 6DE
Tel: 96795 230871
Fax: 96795 230858

FASHIONS for YOUR VIDEO

I (PRINT NAME)   ....

Of (PRINT ADDRESS)   ....

....

....

ROLE in PRODUCTION ....

Do hereby warrant that I will not pass on any details of the content of this programme to a third party, and will disclose any conflicting interest I may have with a similar company. By signing this contract I understand that I am legally bound to respect the need for confidentiality.

DISCLOSURE (If None, write NONE)

Signed:

Date:

to declare that, for example, they are working part time for the opposition. This would then give Ace Productions the opportunity of excluding that person from taking any part in the production.

Poppy prints three copies, signs one and leaves one each on Simon and Elaine's desk.

When she comes in on Monday she will have to organize the catering for the shooting day at Fashions for You, the supplier order for the college catering and the two days' post production catering. There will be a meeting to arrange for Elaine and Mr H to review the voice-over tapes. She will have to arrange to have the banner delivered, and make the arrangements for the clothes from Fashions for You.

Production planning

It is now Monday 13th September. Elaine went to see Richard on Friday and has selected three voice-over artists that she thinks are suitable. Richard has made up a cassette compilation and she needs the final approval for one of them from Mr Hermandes. Why can't she make her own mind up?

Poppy has arrived, offered to make them all a cup of coffee and is looking at her 'to do' list.

Fashions for You Video. Things to Do. 9th and 13th Sept 99

✓ *Confidentiality Clauses for Simon, Elaine and me. Photocopy for*
   Naomi and then file.

✓ *Contracts and Confidentiality Clauses for girls. Post.*

✓ *Julian's cheque. Update Prod diary and post.*

✓ *F for Y cheque. Update prod Diary and pay in to bank.*
   Arrange Meeting for Elaine & Mr H for V/O approval. Cassette?
   Organize catering for 21st, 5th, and 6th. Check numbers.
   Phone college catering, check OK at £60 and send order.
   Ring Hang it All and arrange banner delivery.
   Ask Elaine if she will mention clothes to Mr H.
   Ask Elaine if she wants catering for off line days.

She decides she will see Elaine before she gets busy with her day and ask if she will see Mr H about the clothes and if she has a preferred day or time for the meeting. Then she will work through the rest of the list.

Production planning is all about thinking of everything that needs to be done, or anything that might crop up, and planning to deal with it before it happens. That way everything goes smoothly. You will see that while Poppy was at the meeting on Thursday she wrote down all the things that she was asked to do. She knows that her head is a notoriously stupid place to keep things! People do forget, you can get brain overload and, anyway, isn't it better to be methodical and professional by having a list of things to do; less stressful for you and impressively efficient. Of course her notes will eventually go into the production diary under 'Production planning'.

Elaine has agreed to ask Mr H about the arrangements for the clothes, and would like a meeting as soon as possible. Poppy asked why she needed to ask him about the voice-over. The answer was very simple; it is exactly the same as the music track. If the client makes the decision he cannot complain later and want it changed. We have already mentioned that this is a form of 'insurance'; if you ask the client to agree important things like choice of voice, girls and the music it is his responsibility to pay for any subsequent changes.

An example of thinking about things that might crop up is that Poppy is currently with Simon. She has had an idea. She wants to ask Simon how many people to cater for and if she should ask the college if they could do some sandwiches for the other shooting day and the off line and on line days.

Simon is looking at the budget and modifying it to reflect the extra £100 from Naomi for the extra girl and the extra trouble. He thinks it would be a good idea to ask the college about the other days, but what about tea and coffee? He has allowed £40 for the Fashions for You shoot and £60 for the four days of editing. There will be the three of them and two crew at F for Y, three for off line and four for on line. It can't do any harm to ask, but don't spend all the money!

He also asks her to check that the college know there will be ten people directly involved in the college shoot.

Poppy has contacted Mr Hermandes' secretary and arranged a meeting for 3 p.m. She will contact Naomi to see if she is free, otherwise the tape may need to be left. Poppy doesn't forget things; she also checked that they have a cassette recorder.

Do you remember that Mr Hermandes is not actually the client? He has taken out his own 'insurance policy' by making sure Naomi (who is the client) makes the decision about the voice!

The catering manager said that he was catering for 15 on the Wednesday. When asked about the other days he got his calculator out and said that he had arrived at the £60 because he charges £4 per person. Poppy gave him the numbers involved and he added it up to the equivalent of 19 people. That comes to £76 but he was prepared to charge £125 all together provided they collected the sandwiches at 8 a.m. on the other days involved. He said that tea and coffee was no problem because they could borrow two of his urns and he would supply tea and coffee bags and lots of plastic cups.

Simon was very pleased with this. He asked if Poppy could do the collecting and take them on to the venues. More modifications to the budget!

Poppy organized and sent the order and then continued with the rest of her list.

She will be gone by the time Elaine gets back so she will leave a note for her explaining the arrangements for the catering and the banner.

These are busy days for Ace Productions. Production planning is critical to success. Remember 'planning and preparation make a successful production'!

Camera scripts

Wednesday September the 15th. There is less than a week to the first day of shooting. Naomi was able to make the meeting, after some discussion it was decided to use George Riley for the voice-over. The clothes are being selected and will be brought to the college by Naomi and Mr H, both of whom want to come to the college shoot. The banner has arrived. The catering is arranged. It is Poppy's last day before shooting starts.

Today she will work with Elaine on the shooting script, camera cards, call sheets and prepare the camera logs.

A shooting script is an important document that is part of the planning stage. Strictly speaking it should be used for all productions, but the truth is that it is only really of any use with multi-camera productions, such as studio work, and doesn't really apply to this one.

Once we have the storyboard approved, we can translate it to the shooting script. This is similar to the storyboard but without the pictures. On the left hand side are the shot number and written instructions about the shot using the known abbreviations. The middle of the page is given over to the words that will be spoken, and any instructions for performers. The right hand side will have notes for the sound team about music or effects. At the appropriate point in the script there will be a horizontal line with a slash mark to indicate the cutting point to the next shot.

Whereas the storyboard was a document, generated for the client, that showed the programme in words and pictures, the script is the first of the 'technical' documents designed for use by the director and the various teams in the production. Because it is part of the production planning process, and you will inevitably have to produce one for your coursework, I have used an example from a typical production. It is an extract from a drama shot in studio using three cameras.

If you look at the diagram of the script you can see that we are on shot 13 and shot 14 is cued by the words 'Good holiday?' At this point we cut to a two-shot of the two performers (Bob and Lucy) and the words spoken are 'I've had better,' and so on. The camera cuts to the next shot (shot 15 on camera 2), which is a medium close up (MCU) of Lucy, at the slash mark after 'fault.' You will also see that Bob 'Would you like a drink?' and Lucy 'What did you want to tell me?' are in square brackets, this indicates a stage direction which is explained under the script by (*simultaneously*).

After the medium close up from camera 2 and close up from camera 1 (shots 15 and 16), camera 2 moves to a close up (CU) in shot 17 and camera 1 pulls back to a medium close up (shot 18).

Shot 19 is back to camera 3's two-shot.

At this stage of the script the only instructions for sound are a bottle opening and drinks being poured over shots 17 to 19 and these appear on the right hand side of the page.

BRIEF ENCOUNTER				page 3
Shot No.	Camera	Type	Script	Audio SFX
14)	Cam 3	2shot	Good holiday?/	
			LUCY: I've had better.	
			(*Pause*)	
			[BOB: Would you like a drink?] [LUCY: What did you want to tell me?] (*Simultaneously*)	
			BOB: I apologize.	
15)	Cam 2	MCU Lucy	LUCY: My fault/	
			BOB: What did you ask?	
			LUCY: I just wondered what it was you	
16)	Cam 1	CU Bob	wanted to tell me./ We agreed not to see each other again . . .	
17)	Cam 2	CU Lucy	BOB: (*Agitated*) I know but...../	*Bottle opening*
18)	Cam 1	MCU Bob	LUCY: You seemed to mean it./	
			BOB: (*Annoyed*) Something has cropped up.	
19)	Cam 3	2shot	(*Pause, then composed*) Have a drink./	*Drink poured*

Studio camera cards

If you are involved in a multi-camera shoot of this type the next stage is to generate camera cards.

From the script the director and the camera team will work out which camera will be responsible for which shot. Individual cameras are not concerned with what the other cameras are doing or what the sound people are doing, all they need is a simple list of which shot numbers they are responsible for and what type of shot it is. We will use an example from another part of the script we have just looked at.

You will see from the diagram that this is a camera card for camera 3, and you can see that the camera has some establishing long shots (LS) at the beginning (shots 1 and 3), then tightens into a two-shot (both performers), to follow the interaction between the two performers (shots 8, 11 and 14). When they stand up, and Lucy walks out, the camera has a movement as it pans right to accommodate the movement of Lucy (shot 21). The camera goes back to its long shot (LS) at shot 26 and has a medium long shot (MLS) of Lucy as its final shot (shot 31).

This camera card will be clipped to camera 3. During run throughs and rehearsals the director may change the shot slightly, or even change the camera! It is wise, therefore, to leave space beside, and underneath, each shot so that the cameraperson can make notes of the changes.

It takes, on average, 8–10 years of training and working as an assistant before you can become a cameraperson. One of the reasons for this is that you need to gain an instinctive feel for a programme, the director's ideas and the performers' movements.

You will have been taught what a mid shot (for instance) is. It is only with experience that you can frame it in the most flattering and creative way. Many a director will have to say 'camera 3 – tighten it a bit', or 'camera 3 – loosen it a little'. If the director has to frame all the shots during a run through frustration will set in among performers and crew, time will start getting away and money will start being lost.

It is only when you hear 'camera 3, that's great', or 'camera 3 – just perfect, again' that you can say that you have arrived as a camera operator. This instinctive feel for a shot dictates the overall quality of the programme. How often have you thought 'Great direction – shame about the camera work (sound or lighting).'

Like anything you enjoy you will strive for perfection. There will be those on your course already that you think are great on sound or lighting, or even directing. They probably enjoy it enough to want to make it their career, just as there will be some who really want to do the paperwork and the production planning side that this book is concerned with!

Camera 3 Shot list

Shot No.	Description
1	LS of whole set
3	LS (as shot 1)
8	2 shot Bob and Lucy
11	2 shot (as shot 8)
14	2 shot (as shot 8)
21	2 shot (panning right as Lucy walks)
26	LS shot of set (as shot 1)
31	MLS Lucy

Floor plans

An important part of the production paperwork is to prepare accurate floor plans. For studio work this will involve drawing the various sets onto an accurate plan of the studio area.

Once the set is outlined we can then draw in the position and type of lights that will be used to illuminate that set. The storyboard will give us a rough idea of the position of the actors and the angles of shot each camera will use. Lighting and cameras can now be drawn in to indicate the initial positions the director will use.

These floor plans and lighting plans are drawn up by the director in conjunction with the heads of the scenery and lighting teams. The thinking behind these plans is that studio time and performers are very expensive, the more planning that can be done away from studio the easier and quicker it will be to set up prior to the shoot.

As the director rehearses the actors, camera positions and lighting may need small adjustments, but not a major re-rig. The camera team and lighting team will have time to make small changes and note them on the plans.

I have borrowed a studio plan from a previous Ace Productions' programme. You will see that the studio plan has got as far as placing part of the set and three of the lights. The camera positions and performer movements are not yet shown.

The difference between studio and location plans is that studio tends to have larger, more complex sets, perhaps a whole ground floor of a house, and very many pre-positioned lights, leading to shots being taken in a linear fashion by many different cameras in different positions; leaving minimal editing to be done later.

The location plans are derived from the plan that was drawn at the recce stage. Location uses small areas where the shooting takes place, the lighting has to be brought in and rigged specially. This means there is a tendency to have a plan for each position that contains all the shots for that position. The position moves and the whole procedure starts again. The shots are gathered by one camera in a non-linear order and then assembled into the correct order at the editing stage.

Elaine is hiring in lighting for her locations. What she and Poppy are going to do now is work out which shots belong to which position so that they can draw a simple position map.

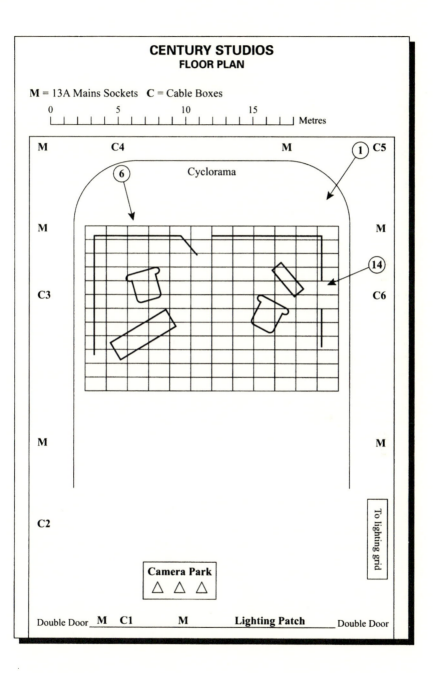

It is normal for location lighting to use very few lights and an experienced location lighting person, looking at a small set for the first time, will have no trouble rigging these very quickly.

With only one camera working from a fixed position the whole operation becomes very much more simple.

The college shoot becomes a little more complex because it is using the theatre and the lights are already rigged. There will be two cameras and a simple set consisting of the catwalk. When Elaine has worked out her camera positions, which she can do from Simon's recce plan, it will be a simple matter to light it. With any luck the theatre crew will already have positioned them roughly in order that the girls can rehearse!

Location shooting script

Time on location is very pressured. You really don't want to 'keep trying shots out' which is why you must plan it out first.

Being on location will mean keeping a very tight control over time. The golden rule with single camera production is to only visit each location once. This might seem very simple but it involves breaking the programme script into a shooting script.

A shooting script details all the shots that are required at each location, no matter where they eventually end up in the programme. In other words the programme is shot in a totally non-linear fashion.

The starting point is to go through the script and pull out each shot that occurs at the same time of day. This is further broken down into which shots are at each location, and this time of day. The next stage is to narrow these shots down to which shots take place at what time with the same performers. We now have an efficient use of time and people. The right people can be gathered at the right location for the right amount of time.

The problem with shooting like this is the need for continuity. With drama programmes the action may take place over weeks, but the shooting takes a matter of hours. The PA will not only need to keep a very close watch on the accuracy of the obvious events like performers ageing, scars healing or 'daily' changes of clothing but also the less obvious, often noticed by the viewer, like the time on the clock on the wall never being the same as the wristwatch that can be seen on a performer, or something in the background that should not be there, a blockbuster period drama film recently had a vapour trail from a jet move slowly across the sky!

With the Fashions for You programme, Simon could have booked the crew for a month and worked his way through the shots in a linear order from 1 to the end. Everybody gets involved in shot 1 at the factory, jumps in the car and goes to the college for shot 2, rushes off to the design studio for shot 3 and so on! Not very clever and prohibitively expensive.

The Fashions for You programme is different to the drama example above. What we need here is to go back to the storyboard and pull out all the shots for each location. These will then form the basis of a shooting script for each location. When we have done that we can shuffle them into an order, which means we shoot all the shots required from one camera position before moving on to the next.

What Elaine and Poppy are going to do now is exactly that. If you looked at the sections on recces (pages 92 and 99), you will now see the reason behind Simon's time saving section on his recce form. Do you remember that he listed all the shots at each location?

Poppy will get the recce forms out of the production diary, copy the shot numbers down for each location and give them to Elaine who, as director, has responsibility for the shot composition. She will decide the order they will be shot and tell Poppy who will construct the location shooting script.

Here is the section of Simon's recce form for the factory location, complete with the shot numbers. You will remember that Simon put them

Ace Productions. Recce for *Fashions for You* .... Date....*10/8/99 p.m.*

Client Name ....*Mr Hermandes*............. Phone No .... *376281* ....

Exact Location .... *Factory - Unit 14 Wandle Bus Pk. - Smithies* ....

Location Contact Name....*Linda Swallow*..Phone No .... *0842634899 Ext. 214* ..

To be used for Shot Nos. ..... *2, 7, 9, 12, 15, 19, 24, 27, 30/31, 33, 42/3, 47* in as he was familiarizing himself with the shots required at this location. It would have taken Poppy an hour or more to go through the storyboard and do the same thing, wasting time Ace Productions is paying for.

There will be one shooting script for the factory, one for the design office, but two for the college. You will remember that Ace Productions is taking two cameras to cover the catwalk sequence. To avoid both cameras ending up with identical shots, each will have their own type of shot to cover.

This is typical of the difference between location and studio. The location cameras have instructions, rather than camera cards, like 'concentrate on the close ups', or 'you are responsible for all the long shots'. Imagine 24 cameras at a football match all giving the director the same shot! Each camera will have been given instructions as to what area they are responsible for. The director's job is to pick the most appropriate shot for the action at that moment. Poppy is working on the factory shooting script (opposite).

You can see from this one page that Elaine has set up three camera positions. All the shots relating to one position will be done together, then they will move to a different position.

Elaine will have the storyboard with her to remind herself of the shots. Poppy will have the shooting script to tell Elaine which shot to do next.

I do not need to remind you that this is not the only location shooting script in the world. You may choose to do it all completely differently. What you must do is to ensure that you maximize the time available and minimize the setting up, shooting, moving position and setting up again.

Camera logs

Logs are the actual record of what was shot, in the precise order it was shot, with details of that shot, which take of that shot it was and which roll of tape it is on. Logs will also often detail whether the take is totally useable, or if only the picture or sound is satisfactory.

There are two logs commonly used, one is the shooting log (a record of what was shot) the other is the edit log (a record of what should be edited to produce the final programme).

FASHIONS for YOU. FACTORY LOCATION. 21st Sept 99 P.M.

Unit 14, Wandle Business Park. Smithies. – Linda Swallow. – 0842634899 Ext. 214

Shot No.	Description.	Instructions

POSITION 1.

Shot No.	Description.	Instructions
2.	MLS Working on Shirt	Shows 4 people (Front view)
19.	MLS Working on Slacks	Shows 4 people and zooms in to MS of Person D working (Front view)
47.	CU Stitching Shirt	Start BCU zoom out to show hands guiding material (Front view) Person B

POSITION 2.

Shot No.	Description.	Instructions
9.	MCU Cutting Material for shirt	Over Shoulder shot Person A
15.	MLS Pattern and Material on bench	Angled over shoulder shot. Person D
30.	MS Sewing band onto skirt	Over Shoulder Person B. Zoom in to show work

PLAN

```
                              ↓
  ┌──────────┐   ┌──────────┐  ┌┘
  │ Person A │   │ Person C │ ←┘  Position 3. (Track round)
  └──────────┘   └──────────┘

  ┌──────────┐   ┌──────────┐
  │ Person B │   │ Person D │
  └──────────┘   └──────────┘

  ↗
Position 2.
                    ↑ Position 1.
```

Programme: Fashions for You. **Director:** Elaine Booker **Location:** Design Studio

Date: 21st September 1999   **VideoTape Number:**

SHOOTING LOG

Shot No	Description	Take	TC in	TC out	OKorNG	Notes

The PA will compile the shooting log on location as it occurs. It is a matter for individuals to decide its exact format but a typical one will have the name of the production, the director, the location, the date and, most important, the tape number at the top. Five or more columns will follow this. Within the columns will be the shot number, a shot description, the take number, the start time of the take (this should be the actual time code time if available or the real time from the start of the tape if not), the shot length, and whether the take was useable or not – this is often shortened to OK or NG (no good). If a take is marked NG it helps to know why. NG Cam would mean that the picture is un-useable, but the sound could be OK; NG Sound would mean the picture is useable but the sound isn't. Apart from these main columns many PAs will have a 'notes' column, for instance it may be that a shot that failed might contain a possible cutaway, or some possible ambient sound. Often when a director calls a cut a performer will relax and may provide a useful smile or a demonstrative movement that could be useful at the edit stage.

The second log is the edit log, which we will deal with at the post production stage.

Poppy will find the shooting log template on the computer, modify it for this programme and then print some out. Time is running out and she still has the call sheets to do. It is nearly 3 p.m. on the 15th, Poppy's last day before the shoot. She will have to go very shortly. She suggests to Elaine that she would like to stay on, in her time, and complete the call sheets. Elaine knows this will take close to two hours and goes to see Simon.

They resolve to accept Poppy's offer on condition that she lets them buy her supper afterwards. Simon is still checking the budget and suggests to Elaine that they have her for three hours on the morning of the 20th to get everything ready for the shoot. More budget modifications for Simon and a happy Poppy!

People in this business do get quite possessive about their programmes. They are living, moving things. Something that you have created and formed for someone else. It is very easy to get tied into this activity and growth, forgetting the simple things. Simon has had the budget sheets on his computer now for three days; as things change they must be entered. It may only be another £15 for Poppy, but now there is supper as well. Does it come out of subsistence, contingency or will you pay it out of your own pocket? You aren't making enough money for yourself as it is, are you?

Call sheets

Whether you are shooting in studio or on location, performers and crew need to be called to be at the shoot when required. The call sheet is a document that will detail who is required where and when on a particular day. There is no standard form this should take, you cannot go out and buy a pad of call sheets. Normally the performer or crew will get one call sheet for each day. Only if nothing changes can you put down 'required for 2 days'.

Apart from the name of the production, the director and the date, the information needed is best thought of by answering a few questions. Who is to go? Where are they to go? How do they get there? What time are they required? Who is the named contact? Is there a contact phone number? What do they do when they get there? What time can they have a break (lunch for example)? What time do they leave? For crew call sheets there may be additional questions to be answered: are there any technical requirements (special make up, props, extra lights, etc)? From these questions it is simple to see that it would help if the call sheet was broken into a 'diary' style document showing times against events, like arrive, shoot scenes 3, 52, 12, 9 and 6, lunch, leave. It may help to have a map showing how to get to the location and certainly needs a point of contact should anything go wrong.

It may be that crew and/or performers are called to a daily production meeting early and then all go to the location together. If so this should be shown, but there is still a requirement for 'what is happening throughout the day' and a contact person and phone number.

Ace Productions find it simpler to break all of this down into two sheets. One is the call sheet and contains information about the programme, the time and place that the recipient is required, a map showing the location and contact names and telephone numbers.

The second sheet is the day schedule. This is effectively a time sheet showing what will happen and when; breaks are shown as approximate times.

For simplicity everybody gets the same sheets, but there is space at the top for the appropriate name to be entered and any special instructions for that person.

For complicated programmes, with lots of special instructions, a photocopy of each call sheet goes in the production diary; simpler programmes, like this one, have one copy and a list of recipients only.

CALL SHEET

For the Attention Of: Camera Operator, Winston Davis

Special Instructions: Meet at Ace Productions. 39, West St. Genie Town.
AT 8 A.M. FOR CREW MEETING.

PROGRAMME TITLE:	Fashions for You Video Presenter
SHOOTING DATE:	Tuesday 21st September 1999
SHOOTING TIME:	9 a.m. to 6 p.m.

DIRECTOR:	Elaine Booker
PRODUCTION MANAGER:	Simon Kent
P.A.:	Poppy Ingles
CAMERA:	Winston Davis
LIGHTING:	Nigel Singler
PERFORMERS (LOCATION 1)	Graham Watson
	Judy Welch
	Joy Anson
	Francis Harty
PERFORMERS (LOCATION 2)	Charles Moss
	Debbie Singer
	Eva Bennett
	Lesley Potter

LOCATION 1.	Fashions for You, Design Office
	21, Gothic Rd. Genie Town
LOCATION 2.	Fashions for You Factory
	Unit 14, Wandle Business Park. Smithies

CONTACT TELEPHONE NUMBERS:		
	Ace Prod.	96795 230871
	Loc 1:	96795 643291
	Loc 2:	08426 34899

SCHEDULE

PROGRAMME TITLE:	Fashions for You Video Presenter
SHOOTING DATE:	Tuesday 21st September 1999
SHOOTING TIME:	9 a.m. to 6 p.m.

Time	Activity	Required
0800hrs	Crew Call at Ace Prod	Director, Prod Manager, P.A. Camera Operator, Lighting
0840hrs	To Location 1	As Above
0900hrs	Set Up Position 1	As Above
0930hrs	Rehearse/Test shots	As Above + Performers
0945hrs	Shoot Pos 1 Shots	As Above
1015hrs	Set up Position 2	Director, Prod Manager, P.A. Camera Operator, Lighting
1045hrs	Break (15 mins)	
1100hrs	Rehearse/Test shots	Director, Prod Manager, P.A. Camera Operator, Lighting
1115hrs	Shoot Pos 2 Shots	As Above
1200hrs	Pack	Director, Prod Manager, P.A. Camera Operator, Lighting
1215hrs	Break (45 mins)	
1300hrs	Move to Loc 2.	

See following sheet for Loc 2 Schedule

Poppy has got to originate call sheets for the director, production manager, PA, three crew and twelve performers.

These are the sheets that Ace Productions use. There will be a second schedule sheet for location 2 (the factory) and a third for location 3 (the college). There will be a separate call sheet for tomorrow. You will see that this sheet (page 157) is for the camera operator, his name is at the top of the call sheet with an instruction to meet at Ace Productions at 8 a.m. Where he is required on the schedule his position (camera operator) is underlined. Winston will be posted these two sheets, the afternoon schedule sheet, a map of where Ace Productions is and maps of the location of the design studio and factory.

You may think this is all a bit unnecessary. After all the crew are booked through Bob who has worked for Simon and Elaine a number of times, and they have met Winston before on another production. The performers work for Fashions for You. What's all the fuss? The fuss is that one day there will be a mix up over who should have been dispatched as camera, or what time, or where they should be. Nobody's fault really, we are all human and make the odd mistake. Nobody makes mistakes on an Ace Production programme; it costs money, causes frustration, is totally unprofessional and demonstrates a lack in the planning they pride themselves on.

The day before the shoot

Some will say that this is the most important day of the whole production. It is the last chance to ensure that everything will go smoothly. Anything missed now will cost money.

Poppy and Elaine are running through the things that must be done today, no one will be in the office tomorrow, or the next day, except for a very brief meeting at 8 a.m. Poppy is making a list of things to do.

You may not agree with everything on her list, or you may feel she has left something out. The way Ace Productions do things is their way of doing things. They know from the time they spent on their course that there are other ways and you may feel the same. What is critical is that everything is covered.

Poppy knows that Ace Productions take a 'production box' on location with them. Everything that is needed is filed in this box. They never take the production diary anywhere. It is the only complete record with all the originals. Things like the recce plans, storyboard and scripts are always photocopied.

Fashions for You Video. *Things to Do.* *20th Sept 99*

> *Phone Bob - Check OK Cam & Light 8 a.m. Tapes?*
> *Phone College - Set done? OK rehearse 6 p.m. tonight?*
> *Phone Catering - Collect food, tea, 8 a.m. - Where?*
> *Phone Mr H. - OK for 9 a.m (Design), 2 p.m. (Fact)*

> *Check all contracts returned*

> *Production Box*
> *Lots of Log Sheets*
> *Shooting Scripts*
> *Storyboard*
> *Music Cassette*
> *Lots of Confidentiality Clauses*
> *Recce Forms and Plans*
> *Copy of Insurances*
> *Contact Phone Numbers*
> *A4 pad, pens, pencils, ruler*
> *Stopwatches*
> *Banner*

> *Double check with Simon & Elaine*

There is always the worry that people might think you fuss too much by ringing up and checking on something that has already been agreed. Ace Productions would rather be certain than have unforeseen worries on location.

What if somebody at the college had asked someone else to ring and say the rehearsal couldn't be arranged, but they forget? What if Bob's cameraperson is ill and he has substituted another? Was the call sheet passed on? So many 'what ifs' that it is no wonder professionals never leave anything to chance, particularly if money is involved!

The 'day before' is the last chance to check everything. Elaine is running through the storyboard and shooting scripts with the recce plans in front of her. She will also make some notes about what she wants to achieve at tonight's rehearsal and about what to say at the meeting tomorrow morning.

Equipment checks

Now is also the time for the technical people to be busy. On your course you will not be in the position of hiring a crew for real money. You will be allocated other course members to do it for you. When Simon was on his course he gave the crew a checklist to follow the day before the shoot; you would be sensible to follow a similar system. Never assume that because something worked the last time you got it out of the cupboard it will work the next time. Things have a very nasty habit of waking up dead! The very best you can do is to make sure that all the equipment you will be taking to the location is working now, you have all the right leads, microphones, lights, spare batteries and a few spare leads. Don't just get the kit out and look at it; set it up and take a few test shots, lit with the lights you will use and record some sound. I had some students once who got to a location, twelve miles away, only to find three of the lights not working and they had forgotten to pack spare bulbs. It is a mistake you only make once.

This is a typical check form for lighting. Simon used it while he was at college. There would be a similar form for sound and camera. Often the director and PA will have their forms. In the case of the Fashions for You shoot, Ace Productions have a 'production box', which has a label inside the top listing the things that will go into it. Poppy has made up her checklist, with Elaine, to ensure that nothing is left out. They know, and perhaps you have yet to discover, there is no embarrassment like the embarrassment that goes with 'Everybody have an early lunch while I just go all the way back to the office to get the storyboard!'

EQUIPMENT CHECK LIST
LIGHTING

No.	Type.	Carry Case.	Stands.	Spare Bulbs.	Working.
2	Blondes	Yes	2 OK	2 (Tested)	Set up & OK
4	Redheads	Yes	4 OK	4 (Tested)	Set up & OK
	Barn Doors	Checked 1 for each light			
	Gel Holders	Checked 1 for each light			

8	Ext. Cables	Plugged in and tested
8	13A to 15A Adaptors	Tested with Meter
2	Multiblocks	Tested

Scrims	4, ½ for Redheads
Safety Glass	All intact, no scratches or cracks
Gel	10, 3,400 to 5,600, 25 various colours
Snoots	Not required
Gobos	Not required
Cookies	Not required

Test Meter	In toolbox
Tool Kit	Checked - In toolbox
Gaffer Tape	2 rolls
Masking Tape	2 rolls
Electrical Tape	2 rolls
Fuses	10 - 13A - tested with meter

Additional Items

Checked by: _____

Rehearsals

Simon and Elaine are going to the college to see Sally Beagle. They have a number of confidentiality clauses that Poppy left because she thought it would save time if they could be signed tonight.

If you are going to follow the proper rehearsal route then you must budget for it. It will involve you in a lot of time and may involve more expense than you think. The performers, for example will need paying and feeding.

Some programmes will follow a fixed format; interviews, discussion programmes and weather forecasts would fall into this category and they will follow the same camera positions and shots and the same type of stage layout each time they are made. It is only necessary to make sure everybody on crew knows the basic format and a short, basic rehearsal is carried out in studio prior to shooting.

For drama programmes several rehearsals will be needed. The early rehearsals are often carried out in rented church halls (hence the need to cost it into the budget). The floor will be chalk marked with the positions of walls, doors, windows and so on; there will often be basic props, odd tables and chairs, for example, rather than the ones that will be used in the final programme. The director and performers will use this opportunity to get to know each other as well as running through their lines and movements and the director's personal interpretation of the plot.

These rehearsals may take days. Gradually the programme will be built up and the shooting script will be refined. Ultimately there will be a final pre-studio rehearsal at which the main technical crew managers will be present to gauge the possible lighting, sound and camera requirements.

All the crew managers will draw up plans, based on what they see, to help with the swift early positioning of the set, lights, microphones and camera positions in studio. Naturally all of these plans are built up as floor plans and will go into the production section of the production diary.

When this early rough set up has been carried out the performers will be introduced to studio. The director will first introduce them to the set and ask them for a dry run, when the watching crew see the actual movements. A stagger through when the camera positions and shot sizes are finalized will follow this. This will translate to the final camera cards and tweaks to the lighting and sound, all documented and filed properly in the production diary, before full rehearsals start.

Much the same happens on location except that the action stops and starts with changing shots, which are shot out of order. The director may use the actual location for rehearsals or, with a complex period drama, may go through the same early procedure of studio rehearsals and hire a hall. The final rehearsals are actual run throughs of the scene that is going to be shot and, because of the requirement of editing the final programme, these are often shot anyway. This leads to several takes of the same scene but may contain useable shots.

This visit to the college will not be a full scale rehearsal, more a look at the set, lighting and girls and allow Elaine to plan out some movements. Neither the design studio, factory nor college are complicated. It is a question of grouping the shots together, making sure everybody knows what they are supposed to do, having a quick run through and then shooting; hence the need to pull out all the shots involving the same performers, at the same location and same time of day, and compiling a shooting schedule.

Elaine and Simon are very pleased with the amount of work that has been done. The set is very professional, the catwalk is a little too long for television but the girls don't have to use all of it. Simon notices that they have tried very hard with the lighting, and says so, but it has been lit 'theatre' which is totally different to the needs of television. Their lighting person will have no problems changing it, so he doesn't mention it.

The make-up people explain that this is the first time that they have used television style make-up and are a bit worried that the girls look 'a bit flat'. Sally Beagle has spent time helping them and explaining the difference and Elaine is sure it will not be a problem.

They are very excited about it and ask Elaine if she would like them to help out at Fashions for You tomorrow. It isn't a course day and they would appreciate the experience. Simon says he can't pay them, but they agree they only want the experience. Elaine decides she will use two of them.

Confidentiality clauses are explained, handed out and returned. Simon has brought the music cassette with him so that the girls get a feel for the programme and to help them with their movement. They have all met Naomi and Mr H who will be coming on Wednesday and bringing the clothes with them, so the rehearsal starts with the girls wearing their own clothes.

As Elaine watches them walking up and down the catwalk she moves around from one end to the other and then from one side to the other. She is looking for camera positions. She has decided that she will use one camera slightly above the girls at the stage end on the catwalk and the other at knee height at the same side of the catwalk, but at the end. This way she can use a variety of shots in the final programme. She can see that the girls have been practised and rehearsed so often by Sally that they have become a bit less lively than she would have liked. She feels that the reality factor on Wednesday will motivate them. She is pleased with her choice of two cameras, which will cut the need for them to go through the same routines time and again. They thank them all and make sure everybody will be OK for 9 a.m. on Wednesday.

Production briefing – 21st Sept.

After 11 weeks we have finally arrived at the first day of shooting. Now is the time that Simon and Elaine will find out if all the planning and preparation will be converted into a smooth shoot, with no hidden surprises. Of course they know that something will happen, it always does, but it should not produce a disaster like a lost day of shooting.

It is 7.45 a.m. and while they wait for the two crew to turn up, Elaine is looking at the notes she has made. The idea of this briefing is to meet the crew, familiarize them with today's locations, using the recce plans, check that they understand the shooting schedule and generally sort out what will happen. They will also be asked to sign the confidentiality clauses.

Ace Productions like to do all of this away from the client. They don't think it is very professional to have these sorts of briefings in public.

They will have another production briefing tomorrow morning, when they will have another camera operator, and will discuss the college shoot using the recce plans and schedules. It will also give them the opportunity of reviewing the Fashions for You shoot.

Simon, meanwhile, is busy doing final checks of the production box and making sure that everything that is needed has been collected up and is ready to be loaded into the car.

Poppy rings up to say she is at the College and has collected the food and drink. She also has two very excited make-up people complete with their make-up boxes! She will go straight to Fashions for You and they will all meet up in the car park. This is part of the Ace Productions professionalism. Elaine does not like crew, or staff, just turning up on client's property individually. They all wait until she can gather them up and escort them in as a proper video unit.

The crew have arrived and are briefed. They don't see any problems. Nigel, on lighting, had seen his special instructions on the call sheet that mentioned the large windows and has brought some conversion filters so that the lights will be balanced for daylight. Winston is a little worried about the space around the drawing boards, but is sure he can get round it. All four of them have worked together before and Nigel remembers Poppy from a shoot they all did a year ago.

Elaine has very quickly formed everybody into a team with a real spirit. This is the reality of people in this business, she thinks, everybody knows the trials, traumas and long hours and that common factor means they all get on really well together. This is why they are all doing the jobs they are. They like the professionalism and conviviality of it all.

Elaine has been making notes during the briefing and these, together with her original notes will go into the production diary in the production section and filed as 'Briefings'.

It is just after half past eight and they load the cars, have a final check, switch the answer machine on and all go to Fashions for You.

The shoot – day 1

There is a common procedure to follow for the shoot. You will see from the shooting schedule that half an hour has been set aside for setting up at position 1. This is followed by 15 minutes of test shots and rehearsals, before the half an hour allowed for the Position 1 shoot. The shot list for Position 1 has been taken from the storyboard, and confirmed on Simon's recce plan.

The crew then move to position 2 where the whole procedure starts again after a 15 minute break for coffee.

This is a pressured time and the first opportunity to see that all the hard work that has been done is translated into smooth success. As production manager it is Simon's job to ensure that the crew set up within the time frame. It is also his job to ensure that the shoot stays on schedule. If it goes five or so minutes over at position 1, he won't be too worried; but if the shoot starts to slip he may have to build in shorter breaks, or consider the possibility of overtime. This will seriously affect the budget.

Elaine, as director will use this set-up time to talk the designers through what will happen and what she wants. She will only involve the position 1 performers, which avoids confusion. She also has to check that the cameras are as close to the final position as possible, giving her just small adjustments to camera height or angle to work out when they start taking the test shots.

The make-up girls are busy flattening out any shiny spots on the performers faces and hands and checking their hair. They have been taught that this is not theatre, and the designers need to look natural. This means a minimum of make-up so that the camera will flatter them, without making it obvious that they are made-up.

Poppy is busy making sure that the shot list and storyboard are available for Elaine, and that she has her clip board with the shooting log sheets, stop watch and pens. She also checks the clapperboard that will be used to mark the individual takes. Rather than a standard chalkboard model, Bob has sent along a new electronic clapperboard which shows the time code times. This will make her life easier when filling in the log sheets.

Nigel has lit the whole area of the four design tables with two blondes and three redheads. They are all converted to daylight with filters and he has used scrims and frost filters to balance the light and avoid hard shadows.

Winston has his camera set up. All the lights are on and set so he asks Poppy to hold up a large white card for him to check the white balance. He asks Elaine if she can see pictures on the monitor that is carefully placed out of eyesight of the performers. He knows that, particularly with amateur performers, there is nothing worse than shooting people who want to watch themselves on the monitor at the same time!

It is just after half past nine, a few minutes later than scheduled, before Winston offers Elaine his first shot. She asks him to raise the camera a little and tighten the shot. She also moves the designer being used a little further back from the drawing board. There is a slight reflection from the metal surround of the drawing board and Nigel quickly fixes it with a little dulling spray.

She decides not to record yet and rehearses the designer. She knows all the others are listening and watching and this first designer will be very nervous. It will pass in a minute or two, but there really isn't any point in recording this embarrassment.

It is nearly five minutes to ten before they are all ready for the first shot. Simon is concerned they are ten minutes over time, but experience says that they will pick it up, as long as everyone moves to set up Position 2 quickly and efficiently. He often shortens the scheduled time needed at the first position; it is a little trick of his to make everybody feel a bit pressured and heighten awareness of the time early in the shoot. He has found that if this pressure isn't applied early, people can get very complacent at the end of the day, when they are tired, and then the times slip quite badly.

Elaine is going to order the first shot. Because they are not recording separate sound, there is no need to bang the arm of the clapperboard down. Poppy checks that she has written the title, location, roll number, shot number and take number on the board and holds it in front of the designer. Silence is called; Elaine uses a ten-second countdown, the first five of which are spoken out loud with the clapperboard in place. The board is removed and hand signals are used for the final five.

As Elaine anticipated it took a few takes to get the first shot. They had done two or three more shots, when Simon noticed a problem. The banner of the Fashions for You logo wasn't it place. It was supposed to have been in the background of the medium long shots and long shots. Whose fault this was is difficult to determine. Simon is responsible for the sets, Elaine should have noticed it wasn't in the pictures and Poppy, as PA, has the responsibility of checking everything! Realizing that they were running late, everybody got a bit tense, this could have upset the performers and, as it does not look good to be squabbling in public, Simon admitted responsibility and they all get on with it.

This is a 'paperwork' book so we won't follow the whole shoot. You will find other books in this 'Basics' series that cover production, lighting and sound, which you may find helpful.

We will assume that the Position 1 shots have been completed, the crew has moved to Position 2 and while they have a late, and shortened, tea break we will look at Poppy's shooting log.

The shooting logs

This log is of vital importance. At the end of a two-day shoot there may well be eight or ten rolls of tape, containing upwards of fifty shots with probably two or three takes of each.

On location you shoot for convenience not running order; this means that the useable take 4 of shot 1 may be half way through roll 6, while take 2 of shot 2 is at the end of roll 4.

At the off line edit stage it is essential that you can find the useable shots quickly and assemble them in the right order. Edit time is expensive and you cannot spend all day trying to find the next shot. All tapes are, therefore, logged as they are shot.

The exact position of the shot is measured by time. The preferred method is to use time code that automatically records the time in hours, minutes, seconds and frames onto a separate track of the video recorder. This makes it very easy to put any tape in a machine and read the exact time from the track. The Beta SP Ace Productions are mastering onto has time code, but the VHS that Simon will use for off line doesn't. He has arranged to have the original time code 'burnt into' the picture so that he can see it on the screen. This is known as BITC (burnt in time code).

If time code is not available then you have no choice but to use 'real time' involving using a stopwatch to get exact timing from the beginning of each roll of tape. Videotape has a control track, again in hours, minutes, seconds and frames, which can be read by an edit suite. Provided the tape is rewound fully and the control track readout is set to zero, location will be relatively simple. Control track cannot be relied on totally and may be quite a long way out by the end of a roll, particularly if it has been rewound and fast forwarded several times.

Poppy's job as PA is to complete the log. She will write down the start time of the shot, which is confirmed visually by the clapper board, and at the end of the shot Elaine, as director, will tell her whether that shot was useable or not and make any comments. Poppy will take the finish time off the time code on the clapperboard, and the whole thing starts again for the next shot. These logs can run into hundreds of takes and some PAs use any trick they can to make off line shot location easier. Some will use a different colour pen for shots 1–10, 11–20 and so on. Some will list the shot numbers on a particular sheet across the top. If there are lots of unusable takes some will 'red box' the useable one.

Programme: Fashions for You. **Director:** Elaine Booker **Location:** Design Studio

Date: 21st September 1999   **VideoTape Number:** 01

SHOOTING LOG

Shot	Description	Take	TC in	TC out	OK or NG	Notes
3	O/S Shirt	1	00:10:00:20	00:10:03:18	NG	
3	O/S Shirt	2	00:10:04:02	00:10:08:13	NG	
3	O/S Shirt	3	00:10:09:06	00:10:14:21	NG	Cutaway?
3	O/S Shirt	4	00:10:15:06	00:10:24:14	NG	Cutaway?
3	O/S Shirt	5	00:10:29:08	00:10:44:20	OK	
21	MLS Designers	1	00:10:49:12	00:11:11:06	OK	No Banner
29	MLS Zoom In	1	00:11:14:02	00:11:18:14	NG	No Banner
29	MLS Zoom In	2	00:11:21:18	00:11:29:21	OK	No Banner
5	CU Design 3/O	1	00:11:34:11	00:11:48:15	NG	Cutaway?
5	CU Design 3/O	2	00:11:56:08	00:12:18:19	OK	
21	MLS Designers	2	00:12:26:17	00:12:31:05	NG	1 Turned round!
21	MLS Designers	3	00:12:39:08	00:12:59:22	OK	
29	MLS Zoom In	3	00:13:07:06	00:13:11:14	NG	Hand on design
29	MLS Zoom In	4	00:13:21:12	00:13:41:23	NG	Cutaway?
29	MLS Zoom In	5	00:13:57:16	00:14:19:09	OK	
11	CU Slacks	1	00:14:23:15	00:14:46:08	OK	
16	MCU O/S	1	00:14:56:12	00:15:18:14	OK	

If you look at the half filled-in log sheet you will see that Poppy has noted the problem with the banner. It is also easy to see the problems they had with the first shot. Notice too that some of the takes have been marked 'Cutaway?'. This is because, no matter how much planning you do, sometimes one shot will not look right when joined to the next one. A short relevant shot is then inserted between the two shots to make it look natural. The best example of this is the shots of the crowd at a sporting fixture. When the highlights are shown later it is easy to show a highlight, drop into the crowd and back the next highlight. The crowd has been used as a cutaway.

These six shots took nearly half an hour shooting, but only just over five minutes of tape!

The shoot – day 2

The second day's shoot starts with a production briefing. The three crew and Poppy are there. Yesterday was discussed. It did not go too well. They could not pick up the time lost early on, despite a shortened break and Poppy being left to clear the remains of lunch into black sacks, whilst the crew moved on to set up at the factory. The factory took longer to set up than expected and the result was an overrun of an hour. Simon will have to cost this into the budget. By the end of the day everybody was hot and tired and just wanted to go home.

The discussion moved to today and they looked at the recce, set and catwalk plans. The camera operators couldn't see a problem, Nigel, on lighting, thought it might take a while to re-rig and plot the lights. The best thing about the day was that the cameras were working from fixed positions and the lighting would be set for the day.

It was agreed that one camera would concentrate on mid shots and close ups of the clothing and the other would stay with long and medium long shots. The basic format would be to keep the cameras running and cover a complete walk in each outfit three times. Simon would then select the bits he wanted at the off line stage. Poppy would have her work cut out because two cameras means two log sheets. The time code on one camera would be slaved to the other giving the same times on each of the different rolls.

Naomi and Mr H would be present and Poppy would look after them, discouraging them from interfering as tactfully as possible. It was hoped that they would not stay all day, but Naomi was obviously worried about her designs and would not want the clothes lying around.

The production box was checked and they left for the college ten minutes late. They arrived to find that Naomi had rung to say she was running a little late and Elaine and Simon couldn't help but feel a little exasperated. Simon said that if the clothes had not arrived before they were due to shoot, he was billing Naomi for the inevitable overrun.

This is certainly a point for discussion; if the schedule is tightly budgeted, and the client knows it, and the client defaults over something (in this case the clothes) there is a case for explaining it and asking for more money. Any reasonable client would pay, but it is best to be reasonable, rather than demanding, because it may be that they decide not to employ you again. It is a matter for personal judgement whether you take it out of contingency or argue with the client.

As it turns out Elaine is rather glad that Naomi is not here yet. Half the college seems to have turned up to watch, their lighting technician is not getting on with Nigel and the stage crew are arguing about where to put the banner. Diplomacy rather than confrontation seems to be needed. Simon, as production manager, has to sort this one out. He talks to Sally Beagle and suggests that the girls' class are included in the audience plus no more than ten others. The three make-up girls will be busy, as will four from wardrobe. He is sorry but he cannot include the technical crew. The reason he gives is that this is a sensitive shoot, which needs confidentiality clauses signed, and the client would never agree to this many being used as 'audience'. Sally fully understands and agrees that it has got a bit out of hand and she will sort it out.

Simon decides against diplomacy with the stage crew and tells then where he wants the banner! He then sees the lighting technician and explains that Ace Productions have hired the facility and not the crew, thanks him for his time and trouble and escorts him out of lighting control. Nigel is happy again. There are times when you have to be a diplomat and times when you have to be in charge. If you feel that you cannot assert yourself faced with these typical problems, you must practice until you can. Major disaster will strike, probably resulting in a wasted and very bad tempered day, if you cannot control your own production.

Elaine is talking to the girls and Poppy is getting all the confidentiality forms sorted out. One of the students has a part time job in the packing section of a rival company and is told politely that he cannot be present; two refuse to sign the forms because they can't see the point. Poppy asks them to leave and they won't. Simon is called to explain, they still won't sign so he asks Sally to request them to leave. They are her students, not his, so why interfere?

Finally at just after 10 o'clock everything, except the clothes, is ready. Elaine asks for the music to be started and runs some test shots with the girls. Poppy has been asked to phone Naomi. She is told that Naomi and Mr H left five minutes ago so shouldn't be more than twenty minutes.

Remember that this book is about a real programme that Ace Productions did a couple of years ago. All this has actually happened, and is not uncommon. No matter how much you plan, if something can go wrong, it will. It is frustrating and upsetting. These things will happen with your programmes. How will you cope? Do you have the diplomacy and communication skills needed? Did you build the budget accurately, including every single thing? Did you consider contingency?

What has happened with this programme is that a young company is desperate to break into a competitive business and needs clients. Simon knew his budget estimate of £10,000 was accurate, then enthusiasm or the need for work, or a bit of both, has forced a situation where they have had to cut nearly £2000 off the budget and are realizing that it can't be done. It is unlikely that the programme will run at a loss, but already their own salaries have been cut and it may be that they will have to cut them some more.

This is the hard fact of the industry you want to be part of. It may be more sensible to start by working for someone else as crew before you jump into starting your own company.

Elaine breaks everybody for coffee. There is no point in people sitting around doing nothing, and even less in running through the same rehearsals time and again until they are sick of it.

Naomi and Mr H arrive. Naomi wants to show the girls which outfits go together, Elaine suggests she gets one girl dressed first and then while they are shooting she can prepare the second. Finally just over an hour late they start shooting. Simon had anticipated this by effectively scrapping the shot list and giving himself more work at the off line stage. It is cheaper than another day shooting and as long as Poppy has full details of the girl's name (needed for captions), which outfit (needed for continuity), and accurate time code details on the logs he will sort it out later. Not very professional, but he has made a time decision. If he had stuck to the shooting schedule they would have seriously overrun; if he does nothing the whole thing will fall apart.

After this early bad luck the day goes reasonably smoothly. Elaine has a quick run through some of the shots with Naomi who seems very pleased. Mr H says he was very impressed with everyone. The crew leave at twenty past six agreeing not to tell Bob that they overran by twenty minutes.

Naomi and Elaine seem to be getting on really well, she is already talking about finding some money for the retail outlet video and hopes they can do some updating of the programme sometime. It is looking as if it was all worthwhile. The four girls got to choose two of the current season's outfits each and Naomi particularly wanted Elaine and Poppy to have a shirt and some slacks. Simon is thinking of the production budget he will have to deal with tomorrow.

Re-shoots

Re-shoots in a studio programme tend to be called pick-up shots. This is because the very nature of studio is to run whole scenes from one end to another. There should be absolutely minimal editing in studio. As long as everything is going well the director will not stop the action if some small thing goes wrong. The PA will mark it on the log, and at the end of that scene just that one shot will be 'picked up' or re-shot.

Re-shoots on location are taken care of by stopping the action and re-shooting the shot as another 'take'. If it is that simple why do we need to worry about re-shoots?

There are two reasons for major re-shoots involving anything from a whole scene to a whole day of extra shooting. The first is 'operator error'. What should happen is when the picture is shot, the camera operator checks that the record light is on, while sound monitors the quality and level on headphones. In studio it is the tape operator who checks that the machine is recording and the sound operators who listen to the sound on loudspeakers. There are occasions when things go wrong. Just because there is a picture on a monitor it does not mean that the picture is being recorded. Just because the sound is OK in sound control it doesn't mean the record level has been turned up on the video recorder.

The whole point of test shots is to check the whole system is working. You record a little bit of anything and play it back to check. When a shot has been recorded on location, or a scene in studio, you should review the last few seconds and check it is OK. If you get to the end of an hour or so and find there was no tape in the machine you will look pretty silly!

The second reason is director error. It is one of the director's jobs to check the content of the picture on the monitor. They should notice a shadow from a microphone, or somebody walking about in the background. The worst example of this, as I mentioned earlier, was a period drama that had a vapour trail, complete with jet aircraft, slowly passing overhead. It was not noticed until the edit stage, too late to do anything other than call the whole crew and performers back, rebuild the set in a far off country and shoot the whole day again! Apart from the expense, the schedule would not allow it, so it stayed in.

Major re-shoots are only necessary if one of the production personnel or crew have failed. This essentially puts it squarely in your court and you pay!

Final production meeting

It is the day after the shoot. Elaine and Simon are having a final production meeting. Everything that happened on both days is discussed. The notes will go into the production diary. The first two important points are 'What went right, and why' and 'What went wrong, and why?'. It is from these points that they will improve their experience and get better next time. It is a debriefing session.

Once that has been sorted out they will look at what they did about the things that went wrong, and what they could have done differently. What would you have done about the awful start to the college day? Would you have allowed rehearsal time for the design and factory locations? When? Would you have allowed two days' shoot at Fashions for You? How would you have paid for it? Was the PA sensibly and profitably employed? Remember they didn't use her for any of the pre-production, and needed extra time during production. Was the crew directed properly? Could you have handled the problem with the banner on day 1? What would you have done, and why?

Once all this has been sorted out Elaine has to bring the production diary up to date and Simon (and you!) will have to finalize the production budget.

You will see that things are not as bad as we thought. Poppy cost £90 more than expected, but £80 of that is transferred from not using her for pre production. The cast was more because of the extra girl. The crew cost more because of the overtime on day 1, but the graphics, props, tape and phone cost less. Simon knew the subsistence would go up when they offered to take Poppy out to supper!

Simon has come out of production £277 more than budget, but he saved £77 on pre production; so far, Ace Productions are £200 over budget.

Nobody remembered to ask Naomi if the second invoice could now be submitted, and the bills will start to come in soon. Perhaps Elaine will find time to ring Mr H and check that it will be OK.

Tomorrow is the start of post production and Simon has to get the BITC copies organized.

Ace Productions. – Budget – (Estimated v. Actual) – Client Mr Pat Hermandes.

FASHIONS for YOU – VIDEO PRESENTER. BUDGET

BUDGET BREAKDOWN FOR PRODUCTION

ITEM	NOTES	DAYS	RATE	ESTIMATE	ACTUAL	DIFF
Director		2	$100.00	$200.00	$200.00	
Production Manager		2	$100.00	$200.00	$200.00	
P.A.		2	$40.00	$80.00	$170.00	$90.00
Cast	34hrs @ $5	1	$150.00	$120.00	$160.00	$40.00
Music	Modified – now 4		$300.00	$200.00	$200.00	
Graphics	Modified		$125.00	$125.00	$95.00	($30.00)
Camera Crew	1 day 1 – 2 Day 2	2 + 1hr O/time	$500.00	$750.00	$850.00	$100.00
Sound		2	$125.00	$250.00	$320.00	70.00
Lighting	Not needed	2 + 1hr O/time	$125.00			
Staging	Now included in	0.5	$100.00			
Make-up	location hire	1	$50.00			
Wardrobe	at college	1	$50.00			
Location Hire		1	$400.00	$450.00	$450.00	
Props	Reduced		$175.00	$100.00	$80.00	(20.00)
Transport			$50.00	$50.00	$45.00	(5.00)
Subsistence	Modified		$130.00	$100.00	$155.00	55.00
Videotape			$200.00	$200.00	$180.00	(20.00)
Telephone			$30.00	$30.00	$27.00	(3.00)
			Sub Totals $	$2855.00	$3132.00	$277.00

Post production

The post production stage is the final stage of the programme's life. This is the stage where all the different pieces come together to form the complete jigsaw.

The pictures that have been shot will be collected together into the right order, the shots will be trimmed to the correct length, any special effects will be added, the captions will be fitted in and the sound will be mixed together to form the final sound track.

How much actual work, and therefore time, this all takes depends on the preparation work that has already been done. If the storyboard has been well thought out the majority of shots should cut together, without the need for cutaways. If the shooting logs have been properly completed every shot will be found easily and quickly.

Sometimes captions and credits are designed as artwork and will need to be shot. Sometimes they are computer generated, stored on disk and can be played back through the edit suite.

How much work needs to be done on the sound is dependent on how careful you were at the shooting stage. Are all the levels the same? Is the background noise minimal, or does it need adjusting? Has a voice-over been recorded? Are all the effects and music needed collected together and logged?

There are three separate stages to post production. The first is off line editing, followed by on line editing and finally audio dubbing.

How many people are involved will depend on what is needed, and how complex the programme. With a really good camera log you should only need the director and an editor for off line. It helps to have a PA to find the location of the shots, and make up an edit log.

On line will need the director, the editor and possibly operators for the tape machines, graphics and caption generators. A sound operator is normally used to balance the dialogue tracks, but it may be that the PA will produce a sound log instead.

The audio dubbing stage needs the director and a sound operator who will mix the final soundtrack together onto the finished master tape. There may be sound operators to operate the various machines and outboard equipment.

Before any of this can start Simon has to get the BITC copies. You will remember that he has arranged for Richard, who will do the on line edit, to do these for him.

The Beta master tapes have time code recorded onto them and those times are recorded on the shooting logs. It is these times that will be used for the on line edit. Simon has decided to do the off line himself using Ace Productions' VHS edit suite, which has the normal control track counter. What Richard will do is to make VHS copies of the master tapes and 'burn in' the time code in a little box at the bottom of the screen.

The master tapes should be insured against any damage but, even so, they should only be run through a machine the minimal number of times. You should still make copies even if you off line on Beta, keeping the originals for the on line edit. Very often companies will make copies of the original tapes, and store them in a different place, in case anything does happen to the originals.

The original shoot took up eight rolls of tape. This means eight BITC VHS copies will have to be entered onto the post production budget at the agreed £5 each.

Editing overview

Perhaps the biggest advance in video production in the last few years has been in the editing process.

With the rapid fall in the cost of computer memory, the availability of larger hard disk storage space at affordable prices, faster processors and more advanced graphics cards, computer editing is now much more accessible to the smaller video producer. This affordable access to computer technology has given rise to an upsurge in non-linear editing (NLE).

Simon decided to use the conventional machine-based editing instead of NLE. He based this not on cost (there was only some £15 between them), but the convenience of a package deal and the fact that he liked Richard more than Tim. He will find out shortly whether he has made the right decision.

There are three distinctly different methods of editing programmes. The traditional method of linear editing involves the need to copy the required sections of video and audio onto a new tape in the order required. Because the clips are in an order, and of finite time, any later change of mind about the length or position of a clip results in a new copy having to be made. In other words, a whole new edited tape has to be made from that edit point onwards.

Copying tapes produces a loss of quality, which is why it is important that the acquisition is done on the highest possible format, no matter what format you will eventually end up with. Often the original tape is copied to a digital format, edited with minimal loss of quality, and then copied back to the desired end format. This obviously involves the expense of digital machines and editing suites.

The second method of editing, based on the advances in affordable computer technology, is non-linear editing (NLE). This method involves digitizing the source material and putting the files of material into a computer. The programme material can now be formed into a video programme using a computer-editing program. These programs work exactly the same as a word processor (except that they process pictures and sound). Clips can be assembled into the right order using cut and paste techniques. Exactly like a word processor the clips can be added to, the order can be changed, bits can be taken out and so on. Editing can start on the day of the shoot or whenever there is enough material to make up sequences. NLE computer programs will have a range of effects and transitions built into them, doing away with the need for a separate vision mixer and effects processor.

If you are using an NLE system it is very important that you keep to the discipline of programme making. A programme should be designed and constructed at the paperwork stage. NLE is a quicker, more flexible method of editing – it is not intended to be used as a tool for sloppy programme making whereby you can just go and shoot anything and then 'make' the programme using a computer.

The third type of editing is computer assisted editing (sometimes called hybrid editing). With this method a still frame (or sometimes a short clip) of the beginning and end of a scene is 'grabbed' by the computer together with its location on the original tape. This is normally the time code number but less accurately, can be derived from the control track. Each of these clips can then be cut and pasted into a storyboard displayed on the computer screen. Any transitions or effects between the scenes can be selected from the computer and added to the storyboard. Because this method uses a computer program to assemble the storyboard, and cut and paste is available, the order can be changed at any time during this assembly process. When the programme is complete the computer is instructed to make the final programme. It does this by copying the bits held on the source tapes in the right order, adding transitions as it goes, onto another tape.

This may be seen as the best of both worlds. It is possible to use the power of the computer to adjust and assemble the programme until it is the way you wanted it to be, and then use the computer to make the edited copy using the original source material rather than a sub standard digitized version.

Off line edit

Elaine and Poppy will help Simon because editing is a very time consuming process in its initial stages. The various clips have to be accurately located on the different source tapes, checked that they will visually join together and if not what can be done. Maybe a cutaway is needed, but whereabouts on which source tape is it? The PA's log will cut down a lot of time wasting if it has been done accurately, but checks still have to be made to see if the programme as a whole will flow as required. The client will often require a 'rough cut' edit before sanctioning a final version. Complicated mixes, transitions and sounds that need to be added will be agreed and done on line.

Edit suites are not the place to log tapes, try out mixes or play with a series of ideas that may not work. Because of this, editing is broken down into two stages – off line and on line.

Poppy will be busy making up an edit log. The BITC will form the basis of a list of all the required edits in the form of an edit decision list (EDL). An EDL is a list of all the locations for the first and last frame of each scene as they are to be joined together to form the final programme. Off line is normally carried out on the cheapest available system (time is money). An off line edit is the rough-cut edit. It will usually only have cuts between shots with, at best, a caption saying what sort of transition will be in the final version. The sound will be 'as recorded', and will not have been cleaned up or added to.

Because the Fashions for You programme will be largely cut to the specially commissioned music, Simon will lay down (record) the music track first and adjust the shot lengths to fit.

This is the Ace Productions' EDL template.

You will see that apart from the obvious exact location of each shot there is a column for comments and prog(ramme) time. Comments will be used to indicate things that Simon cannot do, with this simple edit suite, like a caption overlay or a multiscreen effect.

Only when they have a version of the off line rough cut edit that everybody, including the client, is happy with can they go to the next (most expensive) stage of on line editing.

The on line edit suite has the ability to make the final programme from the original source tapes and the EDL, which is often fed to a computer which will control the machines, making sure they are at the right time code point for each consecutive shot.

At this stage Elaine, Simon and Poppy work closely together. Poppy has her shooting logs and sorts out the time and roll number for the next shot, while Elaine is working with the storyboard, and Simon, to get the current shot cut to length and check that it marries with the previous shot without the need for a cutaway.

Not until Elaine is happy with this edit will the time code out position of the previous shot and the time code in position of the current shot be noted on the EDL.

You might think that to allow two days for this editing of a five or six-minute programme is a bit excessive. The truth is that there were two days of shooting, eight rolls of tape and some fifty shots, as well as difficult multiscreen mixes, captions and graphics. The 'rough cut' off line version has to be approved by the client and it will be a miracle if no changes have to be made!

Let us drop in on Elaine, just as she completes an edit. We will look at the details of how she sets up and executes the next edit.

The first stage is to find and mark the edit points. This can be done on either machine first, but for this edit she does it first on the record machine.

Ace Productions – Edit Decision List – Page					
Title: Fashions for You – Video Presenter – **Client:** Mr Hermandes					
Shot No.	V/T Roll	T/C In	T/C Out	Comments	Prog Time

To find the first edit point on the record machine Simon presses the play button for that machine on the edit controller. Elaine watches carefully (and listens) to find the exact moment when she wants to cut to a different shot. Actually she overshoots it slightly, so Simon very carefully uses the shuttle control to wind the tape back to the chosen point.

Once the point has been found, the shuttle control is centred and the tape pauses, giving a still picture on the screen. Simon now enters this point into the controller's memory by pressing the 'in entry' button. The controller actually stores the number from the control track display, not the real time code, which is why it is very important to write down the time code from the screen.

Elaine now finds an edit point for the playback machine, in exactly the same way. This is the point in the material that will directly follow the point chosen on the record machine, when the edit is done.

Quite often, when building a programme from new, there is no need to tightly mark the end of the edit. It can be allowed to over run slightly at the end, and then the following edit will crop any excess off the shot. This allows Elaine more freedom for the timing of the next edit.

Once the edit points have been entered Simon will try a 'preview' of the edit. This shows what it will look like (and what it will sound like) on the monitor of the record video machine, without actually committing it to tape.

If it isn't quite right it can still be altered, nothing has been committed to tape. Edit points can be moved, or sound levels adjusted. On complex, or very tightly timed edits, it may be necessary to run a number of previews before Elaine is satisfied with it, which is how the time slips away and two days begins to look more realistic.

Now the moment of truth – if all is well with the preview Simon will press the 'auto-edit' button and this time the edit is recorded. Simon and Elaine will now check that the recording of the edit has taken place, and looks and sounds just as it should, by playing it back from the record machine, or 'reviewing' it. If it isn't quite right it is much easier to redo the edit now, with everything still approximately cued up, rather than later when many other edits could have followed and it may all have to be redone. Only when they are happy can Poppy enter the time codes onto the EDL.

Here is just a small section of Poppy's completed EDL.

Shot No.	V/T Roll	T/C In	T/C Out	Comments	Prog Time
1	*6*	*00:54:16:10*	*00:54:21:04*	*Needs FfY logo overlaid*	*00:00*
2	*1*	*00:21:34:23*	*00:21:39:17*		*00:05*
3	*1*	*00:36:29:11*	*00:36:32:10*		*00:10*
4	*7*	*00:06:14:02*	*00:06:18:06*	*Incl. 48 & 16 for 3Screen*	*00:13*
5	*3*	*00:32:37:19*	*00:32:44:23*	*Add Cap LUCY*	*00:17*
6	*2*	*00:43:26:14*	*00:43:33:22*		*00:24*
7	*2*	*00:36:46:18*	*00:36:52:03*		*00:31*
8	*5*	*00:02:31:15*	*00:02:39:06*	*Add Cap GEORGEY*	*00:36*
9	*1*	*00:12:05:13*			

Ace Productions – Edit Decision List – Page *1*
Title: Fashions for You – Video Presenter – **Client:** Mr Hermandes

You will see from this that the in point of shot 9 has been decided, but the out point has yet to be confirmed. The total programme running time has been noted and is currently 36 secs. It is important to have this column because the time codes are meaningless except to indicate the edit points.

Look at the comments column and you will see that there are things Simon cannot do until the on line stage. Shot 1 will have the Fashions for You logo superimposed onto it. This will be generated in the on line suite and mixed in there. Similarly shots 5 and 8 are the agreed captions for the girls. Shot 4 will be a three-screen shot and include footage from two other shots (48 and 16). Once again Simon can't do this with his limited edit suite, but the correct time codes must be entered or time will be wasted in the on line suite trying to find them.

Poppy needs another piece of paper! Ace Productions call this a 'shot guide'. You may just write down the time codes on the original EDL or you may have a sheet similar to this one. Either way the exact times must be entered somewhere.

Ace Productions find this the easiest method because it gives a visual indication of what is required, as well as the times, speeding up the on line process.

Ace Productions – Edit Decision List – Page *1*

Title: Fashions for You – Video Presenter – **Client:** Mr Hermandes

Shot No.	Final Image	Comments
1	Shot 1. V/T Roll 6 T/C In 00:54:16:10 T/C Out 00:54:21:04 *Fashions for You*	Grow FfY logo out of centre of frame. Start 00:54:16:22 End 00:54:20:16 Needs Cap Gen.
4	Shot 4. V/T Roll 7 T/C In 00:06:14:02 T/C Out 00:06:18:06 Shot 48. V/T Roll 4 T/C In 00:23:18:16 T/C Out 00:23:22:20 Shot 16. V/T Roll 8 T/C In 00:17:03:20 T/C Out 00:17:08:00	Use thin blue dividing lines to divide screen areas. NOTE: shot 48 is slightly less high than shot 16. (cut at Waist.)
5	Shot 5. V/T Roll 3 T/C In 00:32:37:19 T/C Out 00:32:44:23 *Lucy*	Fade in/out caption 'Lucy' in Magenta Start 00:32:38:04 End 00:32:41:16 Needs Cap Gen.

These three shots are simple to do with the equipment used in an on line suite. The thinking behind all the preparation work is that it saves discussions and misunderstandings if the final image is worked out now. Richard, who will do the on line, is only interested in what the time code in and out points are and how the pictures fit together.

Poppy has had to time the original shot and then find the component parts of shot 4 (shots 16 and 48), before Elaine can look at these components on the screen and decide which section of the shots she will use. Poppy then has to copy down the time codes and, under Elaine's direction, draw them onto the shot guide.

Some people will bypass this by writing the information onto the story-board. Ace Productions find it easier to go to on line with all the time codes on an EDL with accompanying shot guide.

This process of finding the shots, logging them, finding the composite shot times and making up the shot guide has taken a day and a half. Elaine has finished up with a rough cut edit that has a music track, but no voice-over, and the base shots, but no composites and no logos or captions.

She has arranged to show this rough cut to the client in a couple of days time and has to do something to make it look a bit closer to the finished product; so, what would you do now? You have 4 hours to either redo the edit, work out how to put in logos and captions and get a voice-over, or you present it to the client, in this rather messy state, and hope that he will understand that it will be OK after on line. What are the changes, if any, you would now make? How will you handle the meeting with this first-time client? Can anything be done? This isn't a book you just read, this is the reality of a production that you will experience before you finish your course. If you start thinking out the answers now you will be ahead of the game. Preparation is everything!

While you think about how Ace Productions have overcome this problem, we will sit in on the client meeting of 10 o'clock on the 30th September.

Client review

Naomi and Mr Hermandes have agreed to meet Simon and Elaine in the Fashions for You boardroom at 10 a.m. on September 30th. Naomi has suggested they allow 2 hours for this meeting. The objective of the meeting is to ensure that they are fully satisfied that the programme meets the criteria discussed at earlier meetings, follows the storyboard faithfully and is considered to be value for money. Naomi has withheld the second payment of 25% of the total, which was due on the successful completion of the shooting, until she has seen the rough cut. This is perfectly normal. The client has judged that the shoot is only successful if the images match the agreed storyboard.

If she is not happy with the images then Ace Productions will have to arrange a re-shoot at their expense, unless it can be agreed that the client has changed her mind about the images she wants; it needs to be proved that these are new shots. You will remember that when we discussed re-shoots we said that this would only be necessary if you made a mistake. A re-shoot can only mean you didn't do the preparation to get the shots you promised, or a mechanical, technical or operator error occurred. On line could be postponed while you spend your money putting the situation right.

Elaine has with her copies of the treatment, storyboard, script and photocopies of another piece of paper from the production diary; do you know which one? Simon has the rough-cut edit, music cassette, copies of the correspondence, and notes Elaine made, between themselves and the client; he also has the contract. One of two things happens at client review meetings; either the client will approve everything, because they have been fully informed all the way through the production process and know what to expect, or there will be some discussion, disagreement or outright rejection.

This is a very important business meeting that must be handled in a business like manner. You cannot load up the video and say 'you are really going to like this'.

All these client meetings start with a few pleasantries, Naomi says she had no idea how complex video production was, Mr H thinks it all went very smoothly, Simon and Elaine agree, and explain that it is so much more pressured when the budget is this tight.

Naomi wants to see the video. Elaine says she would like to explain a couple of things first. She points out that the expensive bit of post production is the on line stage, when all the special effects, captions and logos are added and mixed together. It is also the stage that the audio is completed with the voice-over artist, music and background sounds mixed together. It is for that reason that she has brought two versions of the off line for them to see.

The first is the programme with all the base images in place, is to length and has Simon reading the script using the exact words and placing of the script over the pictures. This will give an overall impression of the final version.

The second is broken down into sections, which she will stop and start, that follow the storyboard and have the composite images cut to length, but as two or three images one after the other; they will of course be made into composites at the on line stage. Wherever the logo occurs there is a timed black passage and she will explain what happens at that point. Similarly where there are captions over pictures, the pictures are there and Elaine will explain the caption.

Now you know what Simon was doing for the last 3 or 4 hours of off line. He used the second audio track on the VHS to record the script; Poppy measured the timing of each phrase and noted the time code numbers corresponding to the pictures and then she found all the tape numbers and time codes, for all the shots and composites, that they had spent a day and a half writing down as the edit progressed, and he simply put together another off line copy. This time he inserted black, where the logo would go, and followed the base scenes with the composites. Because the tape was a true 'rough cut edit' there was no need for music or script. Is that what you thought would happen? You may have thought of something better; as long as it allows the client to see all the shots that will be used, and shows how they go together, that's fine.

The other piece of paper from the diary? The shot guide, of course, so that Elaine can show Naomi how the composite picture will be made up. Remember we don't want any misunderstandings at this stage. Your idea of a three-shot composite, mine, Naomi's and Elaine's are probably all different. Rather than try to explain it, show her!

They all run through the complete version, with the music and script. Naomi seems very pleased. She has the storyboard in front of her and has been glancing down at it. She likes the overall feel, particularly with the music and some of the shots that make it look like a pop video. Some of these shots 'break the rules' (have you been told not to cut on a zoom!), but she doesn't know that. She feels that the thing that is missing is the Fashions for You name which only appears in a few of the shots as a banner, but understands that Elaine will explain that to them in a minute.

They now get down to the difficult bit. They will run through the sections one by one, compare them with the storyboard and shot guide and try to imagine it as a finished product.

It takes just over an hour for 5½ minutes of video. There are a couple of simple questions, but no complaints. They re run the original version because Naomi wants to listen to the dialogue again. She asks if it is too late to change a couple of phrases and put another one in somewhere else. Simon says it is no problem; the voice is not being recorded until next week. Naomi says that she will be more than happy to pass the second invoice this afternoon.

This has been a successful meeting, everybody is happy, there are a couple of adjustments to the script, but nothing major, and the second stage payment has been approved.

On line edit

The off line editing suite that Simon uses makes the picture joins exclusively by cutting, because that's how the switch from playback to record works. It isn't possible to do a partial recording, leaving residual parts of the picture underneath in addition to the new picture – the video machine is either recording or not, and if it is, it totally obliterates anything already on the tape.

With most programmes, however, there may be times when we need, for example, a slow dissolve from one image to another. This cannot be achieved in the simple off line edit suite. To achieve it we need another source machine, whose image can be combined, in some kind of vision mixer, with the image from the first source machine. So instead of one source feeding to the record machine we now have two or more; the vision mixer will allow all kinds of combinations, using images from both the source machines simultaneously, particularly if combined with a DVE (digital video effects) machine.

We need to ensure that the two images we wish to mix together are on different tapes, because we will be mixing from both source machines; you cannot put one tape into two machines! Ace Productions has made a big mistake here. You may remember that, in the preparation for shooting stage, Poppy took the shots required at each location from Simon's recce sheets; Elaine checked them against the storyboard and worked out which shots would be done from the same positions at that location. Nobody checked which shots needed to be on a separate tape, to assist with the editing. Now they will have to be separated before on line can start.

An edit controller will be used which will tell both source machines when to roll. The assumption is that we start with one, which runs for a time, and then we make a transition to the second, which continues to roll for the rest of the edit. This process is known as an A/B roll, with the first machine to roll being called A, the second B. Because the timing of the changeover needs to be specified as well as the start and finish times of the edit, programming such a controller is more complex than for simple two machine editing.

We also need to plan, and maybe programme into the controller, the kind of transition we want to happen between the machines.

Remember though, that although we can now have a mix between shots as part of an edit, the record video machine will still only be able to start (and finish) the edit as a cut. With no further apparatus we can alternate cuts (starts/finishes of edits) and mixes (or other effects).

On ordinary, cheaper, edit suites operating on control track pulses, there is an accuracy of about plus or minus five frames. This is quite adequate for most purposes, but it means if we need to edit accurately, as with the Fashions for You composites, there is the possibility of slippage, which shows as a twitch in movements within the shot. This accuracy can't realistically be improved if the machine relies, to know where it is on the tape, on counting control track pulses.

Time code can solve this problem by allowing totally frame-accurate editing. This is done by giving each frame of the video a unique numerical code that is recorded on to a separate part of the tape at the same time as the picture. It is always possible then for the machine to go to a precise location on the tape, and therefore to edit accurately.

Time code is used as the basic control signal, together with a synchronizer, to allow us the opportunity to lock other video machines, or audio tape recorders to one master recorder, so synchronous sound can be stripped off the video, processed, and then put back completely in sync.

The time code from one of the various machines is designated as the master and read by the synchronizer. The time code on the other machines (the slaves) is checked against the time of the master machine. The synchronizer now compares these times and sends out speed instructions that allow all the slave machines to run, in lock, to exactly the same time reference. The times do not need to be identical, but must be continuous, because it is possible to enter 'offsets' into the synchronizer. We might say 'the time on slave one is 2 minutes and 34 seconds behind the time on the master' and the synchronizer will adjust to take this difference in 'time code' time into account.

Time code must be recorded as a continuous signal from one end of each tape to at least the end of the programme. When it is read back it displays the same figures as the control track (hours, minutes, seconds and frames), but they are the real time as recorded, not necessarily the time from the beginning of the tape. The actual time code numbers are required in the form of an EDL if the choice has been made to do time code editing.

Particularly time-consuming is any kind of process that requires a programme to be re-edited. Because editing is really copying scenes onto another tape in the right order, it is not possible with tape-based editing to put something in between two scenes later. A new edit will have to be carried out from the point of the new insert right to the end of the programme. Unlike film we cannot cut the tape and stick a new bit in!

We said earlier that more and more on line suites are using the process called 'non-linear' editing. What this does is store all the rushes of a programme into a powerful computer, which can then allow the editor to move clips, edit them, cut and paste them, sequence them and often add visual effects to them, all within the computer.

This gives complete freedom to change the order, change the edit type or change complete sequences, very quickly. Nothing is committed until the material is fed as output from the computer, and even then it is possible on some systems to change and adapt the edit. Because the shots are digitized and stored in memory there is no need to use separate tapes for composite shots, or ones that will have transitions other than a cut. All options are open, the NLE suite will allow total freedom of fades, mixes and cuts in any order. Maybe Simon should have gone down the NLE route after all!

Currently, because video pictures of reasonable quality have an enormous density of information, a choice has to be made with non-linear systems between image quality and cost. Keeping high quality pictures needs large amounts of processing power and unbelievable amounts of memory in the computer, and as memory is still relatively costly such high quality systems are still only really available to the wealthiest facility houses. The alternative is to accept some amount of compression (which means reducing the size of the signal representing the pictures) to limit the huge need for memory. Unfortunately compression visibly degrades picture quality.

The interest shown in this new generation edit suite means that video manufacturers, computer manufacturers, and software engineers are all researching quickly and competitively to bring the need for compression down, and the amount of affordable quality up. Before long non-linear editing will become the standard way of editing.

It was for this reason of quality that Simon decided to stay with tape based on line, which he has always used. Perhaps he has a fear of the unknown; perhaps he simply doesn't trust the quality that Tim at Edit-All can offer with a 'medium cost system'. What we will soon find out is whether he made the right decision.

At the moment, there are many affordable non-linear systems that can be used for the time consuming 'off line' edit, allowing freedom to try things out or edit sections shortly after they have been shot. The output quality to tape is only good enough to produce a 'working copy' as a reference, but the system may be capable of producing an EDL to take to an on line, tape based, edit suite. Simon keeps going to trade shows and looking at them – the VHS suite can't last forever – but even a few thousand pounds is too much investment for Ace Productions at the moment.

It is the 5th of October. Elaine, Simon and Poppy are on their way to Richard at First Post for the on line edit. They have with them the storyboard, EDL, shot guide and the modified script. They also have four other forms that will help the on line to go smoothly. The script has been broken into sections and timed, to help the voice-over artist; there is an audio track chart to show the exact placing of the music, voice and sound effects and a list of captions and logos that will have to be made up.

Simon has also had to do a list of the shots that have to be separated onto different rolls of tape, which has not pleased him at all; to make copies of the original material will mean deterioration of the quality and involve using different time code times. The copy will have to be prestriped with new time code.

Rather like the production was broken down into pre production, production and post production, on line is broken down into assembling the graphics, the voice, sound effects and music. The edit suite cannot lay a caption over a picture unless the caption exists. It is quicker, therefore to assemble all the component parts of the programme first, then edit it all together.

Richard has already pre-striped a blank tape with time code and the first thing that he will do is to generate the captions and logo and record them onto tape. He will then have to copy the shots that need separating.

This is part of Poppy's graphics list.

Ace Productions. Graphics Placement List.			Page *1*	
Programme: Fashions for You.			**Client: Mr Hermandes**	
Reqd. for Shot No.	Time	Graphic	Placement	Special Instructions
1	6 secs	Fashions for You logo	Grow Logo out from centre of screen over 4 secs	Start from black 2 secs before mix to shot 1 picture
5	3 secs	Lucy (Colour is Magenta)	Bottom Right	2 secs into shot fade in and out
8	3 secs	Georgey (Colour is Red)	Bottom Right	2 secs into shot fade in and out
14/15	5 secs	Fashions for You logo	Top third of screen	Overlaid over shot 15 and used to wipe horizontally over shot 14
18	3 secs	Sam (Colour is White)	Bottom Right	2 secs into shot fade in and out
21	5 secs	Fashions for You logo	Centre	Rotate for 2 secs hold and fade out
23	3 secs	Zena (Colour is Blue)	Bottom Right	2 secs into shot fade in and out

You will remember that Simon did the rough-cut voice-over himself, while Elaine found the exact position for each bit of script and Poppy noted down the time code numbers. The original storyboard showed the words against the shot numbers, this was then refined into a script which had the shot numbers in one column followed by the script and some instructions. These instructions included things like 'wait until girl is halfway down catwalk. Run over start of shot 15'. This has now been translated into a voice script, for the voice-over artist, who only wants to know what the words are and how long it should take to say them.

There are many ways of recording the voice-over. Often the tape is edited into final form and then taken to audio post production where the voice-over artist will sit and watch the video while recording the right words over the right pictures. Sometimes a script will simply be recorded and pauses inserted later. Richard likes to have the voice-over artist record each segment separately onto a DAT machine, which has been pre-striped with time code. He then makes up a multitrack DAT tape, also with time code, which includes all the effects, voice and music. This final audio copy is then slaved to the master tape and dubbed.

This edit facility has a sound engineer and she will record the voice-over whilst Richard starts to generate the captions. Elaine and Poppy will be with Richard to talk him through the storyboard, shot guide and graphics placement list. Simon is with Sheena and the voice-over artist.

The script is now in a form that can be read easily, which makes the recording simpler. There are a few general guidelines for this recording script. It should be in upper and lower case, double-spaced, which makes it more readable. It also helps if it is in the centre of the page. This ensures that the person recording it does not have to move their head from side to side, aiding recording balance. Often the voice-over person will use all this space to 'mark up' the script; putting in the emphasis points, pauses, intonation and phonetic pronunciation of difficult words. Because Simon wants this script recorded as timed segments, he puts the words in boxes with the time beside it. His recording script looks like this.

It is mutually agreed that Simon will read each section first to demonstrate the emphasis, pauses and pace that is required and then it will be recorded. It will not take very long to record this short script – there is barely 3 minutes of dialogue in the whole programme – and so each section will be replayed and checked before going on to the next.

Meanwhile the others have been busy with the caption generator. It has not taken as long as Elaine feared because the DVE that Richard uses can place the caption anywhere and add any effects necessary.

What is beginning to take time, and cause a bit of frustration, is

Ace Productions.   RECORDING SCRIPT.   Page 4

Fashions For You Presenter.

Segment 12.   The care taken from concept   11 secs
               through to the final design is clear
               to see. *(slight pause)* Fashions for
               You are proud of the exciting
               range of casual trousers, *(slight
               pause)* and of the designer look
               of the product

Segment 13.   The latest shirt design is one of   6 secs
               the Fashions for You best sellers,
               (slight pause) and you can see
               why!

copying the different shots needed for some of the composites onto a new tape and adding the new time codes to the EDL. Richard has to record a few seconds before and after the shot so that the machines can lock up and then Elaine must find the edit points again. They have made a big mistake here, which wouldn't have mattered at all if they had decided on non-linear editing.

The way that Richard had planned out the day and a half of on line was to break it into three parts; half a day on recording the script, generating the captions and mixing some base shots, half a day actually editing from Elaine's EDL, and half a day finishing the sound and making VHS copies. They are going to overrun by about three hours, and now need three edit tapes. Ace Productions will have to pay for this mistake; Simon will have to look at the budget again!

By the time they have stopped for lunch and all the various sections of tape have been sorted out it is just after four in the afternoon. The choice is simple, either they run on into the evening or they start again tomorrow and see how far they get in the allocated half day. Richard cannot run on tomorrow afternoon because he is booked; he could do the morning of the 8th. Elaine and Simon know that is hand-over day; they don't have any choice. Simon wants to know how much it will cost; Richard doesn't know until he finds out how long it takes. Frustration levels are rising and all because they forgot the basic rule that you cannot mix two shots that are on the same tape. They are both also beginning to realize that if they do get the sales presenter programme, and the seasonal updates, they cannot just 'replace shots', or change the order, without a complete re-edit. Another reason to have chosen NLE!

The decision is made. They will run on and aim to finish the edit tonight; Poppy will stay and help out with the paperwork; more over-time!

The groundwork has been thorough; all the time codes are entered into the edit controller, the effects and transitions are programmed in and Richard starts to build the programme. He has laid the music track down as a guide track for the pictures so that Elaine can check that the cuts and mixes happen where she wants them.

Eventually the picture track is very close to completion and the suggestion is made that they go home and come back in at 8 a.m. tomorrow. It is half past nine in the evening and Richard is going to charge another £250.

The audio dub

The next morning Simon and Poppy are with Sheena, the sound engineer. Elaine is with Richard and they are putting the finishing touches to the picture track. Sheena looks at Simon's track chart to make sure she understands it. She uses an 8 track multitrack DAT machine and will lay down the music in stereo first, then put the voice segments in the right place on another track and finally add the applause and any background sounds.

You will see from the section of the track chart that the time code starts at an indicated time of 10 mins. This is fairly normal; most synchronizers have difficulty knowing what to do when they get to 00:00:00:00, hence the often heard caveat of 'never let the time code cross midnight'.

Ace Productions.		TRACK CHART		Page 1
Fashions For You Presenter.				
T/C In	Track	Content	Duration	Comments
00:10:00:00	1 & 2	Music	5 mins 38 secs	Stereo. Fade
				in/out
00:10:26:03	3	V/O segment 1	8 secs	Duck Music
00:10:30:12	4 & 5	Applause	4 secs	Stereo. Under V/O
00:10:42:16	3	V/O segment 2	6 secs	Duck Music
00:11:06:21	3	V/O segment 3	5 secs	Duck Music
00:11:14:06	3	V/O segment 4	8 secs	Duck Music
00:11:15:00	4 & 5	Applause	5 secs	Stereo. Under V/O

Remember this is an example of a track chart. It is the one that Ace Productions uses. Some people find it easier to use a 'tape view' where the time runs along the top and the tracks run down the page as in this example.

Time	00:10:00:00	10:26:03	10:42:16	11:06:21	11:14:06
Track 1	Music Left				
Track 2	Music Right				
Track 3		V/O 1	V/O 2	V/O 3	V/O 4
Track 4		Applause			Applause
Track 5		Applause			Applause
Track 6					
Track 7	Mix Down Left				
Track 8	Mix Down Right				

It is now possible to 'see' how the various sounds overlay each other. You will notice that tracks 7 and 8 have been designated as 'mix down'. This is because all the sounds are recorded at the same optimum level of 0 dbs (the red line on the meters). The final mix will consist of all the sounds that have been adjusted to their correct level for fade ins/outs in the mix.

It has taken nearly two hours to find all the relevant pieces, and assemble them in the right order and right place on the tape. The audio track has now been completed and Sheena marks up the track chart; she needs to be familiar with where the sound level adjustments take place. She tries a rough mix; it sounds OK so they decide to do a final mix to take to Richard and Elaine.

Elaine is very pleased with the final picture track. Richard links the DAT audio mix through the synchronizer, and using the music guide track to ensure it is in sync, they run the final picture and soundtrack to check that everything is in the right place. It looks and sounds very good so a final composite master tape is made, played back as a final check, and Richard starts to make the four VHS copies.

Ace Productions have come out of this fairly well. Simon will be back in the office this afternoon doing the final budget. Elaine will make sure the production diary is up to date. Poppy will be back at the agency.

Budget reconciliation

Simon has got the final figure from Richard. He has charged an extra £250 for the extra evening, used three edit tapes and done eight BITC copies.

The moment of truth is rapidly arriving. Pre production was £77 under budget, production was £277 over budget, largely because the shoot overran and they used more of Poppy than planned. Now the edit has overrun, entirely due to their fault in not separating the shots onto different rolls of tape when shooting.

The question has to be 'how bad is it?'

The situation is not as bad as Simon thought it might be. They went over budget on the PA and on line editing because he forgot to separate the shots at the shooting stage. He grossly overestimated the BITC cost, and that was because he was estimating from old figures. By the time it

Ace Productions. – Budget – (Estimated v. Actual) – Client Mr Pat Hermandes.

FASHIONS for YOU - VIDEO PRESENTER. BUDGET

BUDGET BREAKDOWN FOR POST PRODUCTION

ITEM	NOTES	DAYS	RATE	ESTIMATE	ACTUAL	DIFF
Director		4	£100.00	£400.00	£400.00	
Production Manager		4	£100.00	£400.00	£400.00	
P.A.	36 hrs @ £5	4	£40.00	£160.00	£180.00	£20.00
Off Line Edit	Modified to £100 pd	2	£100.00	£200.00	£200.00	
On Line Edit	Now 1½ days + £250, Quoted 1½ days @ £950		£600.00	£600.00	£1200.00	£600.00
Special Effects	included	0.5	£300.00	£150.00	£0.00	(£150.00)
Voice Over	included	0.5	£350.00	£175.00	£0.00	(£175.00)
Audio Dub	included	0.5	£250.00	£125.00	£0.00	(£125.00)
Telephone			£15.00	£15.00	£18.50	£3.50
Subsistence			£60.00	£60.00	£67.00	£7.00
Video Stock	8 Bitc, 3 edit, 1 VHS		£180.00	£180.00	£75.00	(£105.00)
Transport			£25.00	£25.00	£28.00	£3.00
			Sub Totals £	£2490.00	£2568.50	(£78.50)

page 4

is all correctly budgeted Ace Productions have lost £78.50 on post production. This adds to the £277 they lost on the shoot, again their fault because the failure to notice the missing banner put them into overtime with the crew. This can be offset by the £77 they gained in the pre production stage, largely because they didn't employ the PA.

The position at the moment is that they are over budget by £278.50. It has to be accounted for somewhere so Simon will now look at the budget for indirect costs. You will remember that the lawyer had to be consulted about the confidentiality clause, for which he wants another £50; Naomi recognized that using a fourth girl would cost more in salary and time and offered another £100 which must be added to contingency; Richard charged £10 per tape for the VHS copies.

The indirect costs budget now looks like this:

Ace Productions. – Budget – (Estimated v. Actual) – Client Mr Pat Hermandes.

FASHIONS for YOU – VIDEO BUDGET

BUDGET BREAKDOWN FOR INDIRECT COSTS

ITEM		ESTIMATE	ACTUAL	DIFF
Insurance		£250.00	£250.00	
Legal		£100.00	£150.00	£50.00
Duplication		£30.00	£40.00	£10.00
Contingency		£300.00	£400.00	(£100.00)
	Sub Totals £	£680.00	£840.00	£40.00

The indirect costs budget shows that there is a £40 surplus. All that needs to be done now is to work out a breakdown sheet for the production diary. This last sheet is important because it will show the areas that went wrong, and why. It will also show whether any profit has been made.

We already know that Simon and Elaine had to cut their salaries to be able to lower their estimate enough for it to come close to the Fashions for You offer. Now Simon wants to know if they made any money for the company. It is all very well paying yourself, but what about the rent, electricity, equipment and all the other things that a company has to pay out before it can even start working.

We said earlier that Simon would normally put in an amount for finances, to offset the accountant's bills; he couldn't afford to. Maybe you should consider putting an amount into your indirect costs budget called 'rent and rates', or 'company costs', as well as financial; It would certainly be more realistic.

You will see from the sheet that Elaine and Simon have made some £1500 for three months work, and that is before tax! It isn't surprising that they still need their part time jobs.

Taking the £400 contingency out of the equation, the programme has made a loss of £38.50. This is a very satisfactory result. To balance the books the £38.50 has been deducted from the £200 that was allowed for the hire of their own off line suite.

If we assume that these three months ended when all quarterly bills were due, you will see that Ace Productions made enough money to cover the solicitor, insurance, phone bill, mail, telephone and some of their food. The still have to pay the rent and rates, and the electricity. The profit to the company was only £161.50p. Unless you do work from your back bedroom, rent, rates and electricity for a quarter will be more than there is available.

There are two lessons to be learnt from this. One is that everything must be costed into the budget. There was no allowance, for instance, for stationery. Printer cartridges and paper are not cheap. The second lesson is obvious: if you take three months to do something that you can only charge two or three weeks for you must be doing something else in the mean time. This is true with any business.

Starting a business is a huge financial responsibility. You will be lucky to break even for the first three years.

Ace Productions.   Final Budget Summary   8th Oct. 99

Programme: Fashions for You Presenter

Client: Mr Hermandes

Start Date: 8th July 1999.   Hand Over: 8th October 1999.
Production Time: 13 Wks

	Estimate	Actual	Comments
Pre Production	£2190.00	£2113.00	Didn't use P.A.
Production	£2855.00	£3132.00	Shoot Overtime. P.A. & Subsistence
Post Production	£2490.00	£2568.50	On Line & P.A. Overtime. Forgot to
			separate shots.
Indirect Costs	£680.00	£840.00	Additional Lawyer time. Extra
			£100 in contingency.
TOTAL	£8215.00	£8653.50	£438.50 overspend

TAKING £400 OUT OF CONTINGENCY, THIS PROGRAMME HAS MADE A LOSS OF £38.50p

Elaine Salary		£1520.00	Raise Cheque
Simon Salary		£1590.00	Raise Cheque
P.A. Cost		£350.00	Raise Cheque
Lawyer Cost		£150.00	Raise Cheque
Insurance Cost		£250.00	Raise Cheque
Music Cost		£200.00	Paid Cheque
Cast Cost		£160.00	Paid Cash
Location Cost		£450.00	Raise Cheque
Shooting Crew		£1170.00	Raise Cheque
On Line		£1200.00	Raise Cheque
Tape Cost		£295.00	Included in Shoot & On Line i/v
Graphics & props		£175.00	Paid
Subsistence		£340.00	Petty Cash
Transport		£118.00	Petty Cash
Phone/mail		£85.50	Petty Cash
Off Line Hire	£200.00	£161.50	Profit to Company
TOTAL		£8215.00	Total Cost = Total Invoice Value

It is worth looking at the way this Final Budget Summary has been laid out. This will be the one most important document in the production diary when Ace Productions review the programme costing to gain financial and budgeting experience for the next programme.

They have started by repeating the estimate and actual costs for the four stages they use. Now they have added a comments column to help them understand what went wrong (e.g. shoot overtime, PA and subsistence).

This has led them to use the £400 contingency (which was for just this purpose) to reduce the overall overspend to £38.50p.

The bottom section is a breakdown of what everything cost, including salaries. In the comments column is a note to raise cheques, or in the case of cast, graphics and props there is a note that they have paid cash. The cheques will be issued when the invoices come in and their numbers entered after 'raise cheque'. This cheque number will also be added to the invoice.

You will notice that the tape cost has been marked as 'included in shoot and on line i/v'. For the moment it still has to be costed into the total because the amounts allowed for these items are the agreed figures, excluding the tape stock.

Hand-over and invoicing

8th October 1999. Three months after the first letter from Fashions for You enquiring about a programme, Ace Productions have a programme to deliver in final form. Simon spent part of yesterday copying the programme many times onto the same tape making a continuous programme of just over two hours. This will save rewinding every five or so minutes which, apart from the boredom, will not do the tape any good at all over the period of a trade show.

Simon and Elaine go to see Naomi and Mr Hermandes as arranged. In their briefcase are several things from the production diary. They take the treatment, storyboard, contract and the notes that were made at the meetings with the company. They are not expecting differences of opinion at this stage, but it is better to have these to refer to if they are needed.

Fashions for You are very pleased with the programme. They admit that this was their first venture into video and compliment Simon and

Ace Productions
Video Programmes on Budget & on Time

39, West Street
Genie Town
GT64 6DE

Tel: 96795 230871
Fax: 96795 230858

Naomi Findler
Fashions for You
21 Gothic Road
Genie Town GT64 2TX

8th October 1999

Invoice No. 01237

Fashions for You Video Presenter

Agreed 50% of total cost of programme (£8215)   £4107 : 50

Agreed additional £100 to cover 4th performer   £ 100 : 00

                    Total Now Payable   **£4207 : 00**

Elaine on how smoothly it all went. Naomi asked that the final invoice should be submitted to her personally and she would pass it for payment immediately.

As Simon and Elaine leave Naomi says 'Fernando and myself would like to say thank you for all your hard work; we are sure the programme will help our sales enormously. We look forward to working with you again.'

As they get in the car Simon remarks that Fernando will always be Mr H to him.

As soon as they get back to the office, Simon raises the last bit of paper for the production diary, the invoice.

Post mortem

As I explained in the introduction, what I have tried to do with this book is to help you with two distinct and different areas of video production. One is to understand the paperwork that will be involved in the production process; the other is to try to heighten your awareness of the communication and business skills you will need if you are intending to set up your own video production company.

We have looked at a real programme that was made by a real production company. Two people, who met on a course like yours, have not been in business long and are struggling to survive, run the company.

Your course and, hopefully, this book will help you to make your decisions about what you do when you leave college.

Let us have a quick review of what happened to Ace Productions. It was three months between getting a request for a programme and completion; this is realistic. Both Simon and Elaine earned about £1500 each during this time. The total profit was only some £150. Two things come out of this; maybe you can survive on £500 a month, but where is the next production coming from, and when? The rent for their very small office is £1000 a month excluding the rates, electricity, phone and so on. How do they find that if they only make £150 profit in three months?

Simon, using his previous business studies skills, managed to come out as close to budget as makes no difference. What went wrong? His original estimate was £10,000, which now looks realistic. When he had all the figures he needed it came to over £9500. Doesn't this suggest that his original estimate was accurate? Why did he agree to try to take £1500 off it? Here is the dilemma that demands all your communication and negotiating skills. Do you lower the budget to an unrealistic figure, because you need the work, or do you patiently explain to a client that these figures are realistic and cannot be reduced, risking losing what is, in any event, an unprofitable programme? Simon and Elaine did explain that the programme would be compromised and could not include all the special effects at a lowered price. That would have cut a lot of work off line and, ultimately, the on line cost. They went ahead with the original programme anyway, why?

Because of budget problems Ace Productions left out an amount to cover the accountant's bill at the end of the year. They also decided on £300 contingency, which as we saw, was unrealistic. A normal contingency would be around 10% of the budget. Would you have lowered it? If they had made the original estimate a 'guess' at £12,000 and used communication and negotiating skills to see how far it could be cut, without compromising the programme, then come up with a figure close to £10,500 the client might have been persuaded that he has saved £1500 already, and can't have his programme cheaper. Is this what you would have tried?

The majority of the paperwork was completed during the pre production stage, yet they decided not to employ any help, why? The PA only cost £5 an hour; surely it would have been sensible to have her in for two or three hours three times a week and used her to look after the production diary; but that brings us back to money, an unrealistic budget and poor organization.

The first day's shoot went wrong because they were dealing with a new team of people, amateur performers, and no rehearsal. Would you have booked a half-day rehearsal, with the Hi8, to settle them down and boost their confidence? The overtime incurred would probably have paid for it. Why two cameras, and a whole day, for the catwalk? Was Elaine still thinking studio? Should she have gone to studio anyway and avoided the strife of an amateur setting, with keen, excited, students. It would only have taken half a day in studio. The difference in cost would have been minimal.

Why did Simon decide to go to tape-based on line? They are hoping to get updates and different versions of the programme in the future. Non-linear would have made this a great deal easier, quicker and cheaper. There was no difference in the final price, even if they did have to sort out their own BITC copies and voice-over. Simon was tempted by the package price and the fact that he liked a person he had never met on the strength of one phone call. If you pay someone to do something, you are the employer, they do what you tell them to; liking them is a bonus. There would have been no problem with all the shots being on the same roll with NLE, saving the on line overtime. The programme was ending up on VHS, not broadcast quality; a 'medium range' NLE suite would surpass that quality anyway. What would you have done?

What we have learnt is that your course cannot teach you everything; only experience can do that. The good news is that, now a few years on, Ace Productions have survived. They now employ Poppy full time, Simon has got his NLE suite and it is good enough quality for him to use it for on line when they end up with a VHS master. They did do the Fashions for You retail presenter, and do all the seasonal change programmes. They are also charging realistic figures. Experience has taught them much, but it took four or five years.

I sincerely hope that, whatever you eventually decide, you will have a pleasurable and successful career in this very stressful, but exciting, business.

Glossary

ACTUAL BUDGET – The total actual cost of the programme, most easily composed by using a separate column on the estimated budget sheets.

AIMS – An outline idea of the programme content.

AUDIO DUB – Recording or re-recording the audio components of a programme, without disturbing the picture track.

BETA SP – Broadcast quality high band analogue video recording system (trade name).

BITC (BURNT IN TIME CODE) – Pronounced 'bit see'. A copy of the actual time code taken from the master tape which is visible in an area of the picture.

CAMERA SCRIPT – Script which indicates types of shots required, often includes lighting and sound.

CAMERA CARDS – A shot list for an individual camera. Assists the operator with the composition of that camera's required shots.

CLIENT BUDGET – A breakdown showing the total cost of each area of the programme only.

CONFIDENTIALITY CLAUSE – A clause, within a contract, that legally binds the person named not to divulge anything of the nature, or content, of a programme to a third party.

CONTINGENCY – An amount of money included in the indirect costs of a programme that can be used to cover the unforeseen forcing a programme over budget. Normally amounts to 10% of the total cost.

CONTRACT – A legally binding agreement between two or more parties.

CONTROL TRACK – Separate track on a videotape containing time and synchronization signals.

COPYRIGHT – Everything from a piece of music to a street belongs to someone. It is an offence to use anything without the owner's consent. Often there will be a charge made for its use.

EDIT LOG – A list of time codes taken from the shooting log indicating the position and roll of each shot in the correct order.

EDL (EDIT DECISION LIST) – A list of the exact time code position, roll number and type of transition that will make up the final edit.

ESTIMATED BUDGET – The estimate of the cost of a programme, broken down into the three areas of production plus indirect costs. Must include everything from sandwiches and taxis to crew and performers.

HEALTH AND SAFETY – A legal requirement that requires employers to have a duty of care over their employees

INDIRECT COSTS – The part of the overall budget, which contains items that are not directly related to the production. Legal and accounting fees are examples.

INVOICE – A request for payment in return for services supplied.

MORAL RIGHTS – Term used in copyright law which gives the original author of a work (e.g. script or music) the right to protect his work from misuse, by cropping sections or substantially changing the original concept. Can be waived by signature on a contract.

NLE (NON LINEAR EDITING) – A computer based editing system, which allows picture and sound to be assembled, cut, inserted and formatted as with a word processor.

OBJECTIVES – A precise statement of what the programme will achieve.

OFF LINE EDIT – A rough cut edit to produce a final look to the programme and an editing log. Normally done on low-level equipment.

ON LINE EDIT – The final edit when all the effects, transitions, captions and graphics are added. Always uses the original masters or copies of them in a higher format.

POST PRODUCTION – The final stage of a programme, which will include editing, special effects and audio dubbing.

PRE PRODUCTION – The first stage of a programme's life when all the preparatory work is done.

PRODUCTION DIARY (LOG OR FILE) – The complete record, on paper, of the life of a production. Contains everything to do with the programme from notes to contracts.

PRODUCTION – The actual shooting and recording part of a programme.

PRODUCTION ASSISTANT (PA) – Assistant to the director with responsibility for scripts, logs and continuity.

RECCE – The thorough examination of a location. This involves drawing plans, and noting down all the physical and physiological factors that will affect the shooting at that location.

REHEARSAL – Stages a programme will go through before recording begins.

RUN THROUGH – The last rehearsal before recording. Includes all camera movements, lighting changes and sound effects.

SAFETY LANE – A clearly defined walkway leading to the nearest fire escape.

SHOOTING LOG – A list of the time code numbers for each take and whether it is useable.

SHOOTING SCRIPT – See Camera script.

STAGGER THROUGH – The first rehearsal where technical problems can be judged and corrected.

STORYBOARD – A visual representation of the programme and the accompanying script.

TARGET AUDIENCE – The specific intended viewing audience of a programme.

TIME CODE – A digital signal recorded onto a separate track of audio or videotape giving a precise location in hours, minutes, seconds and frames.

WALK THROUGH – See Run through.

 **Focal Press**

www.focalpress.com

Join Focal Press on-line

As a member you will enjoy the following benefits:

- an email bulletin with **information on new books**
- a regular **Focal Press Newsletter**
    - o featuring a selection of new titles
    - o keeps you informed of **special offers, discounts and freebies**
    - o alerts you to **Focal Press news and events**such as author signings and seminars
- complete access to **free content**and reference material on the focalpress site, such as the focalXtra articles and commentary from our authors
- a **Sneak Preview**of selected titles (sample chapters) *before* they publish
- a chance to have your say on our **discussion boards**and **review books**for other Focal readers

Focal Club Members are invited to give us feedback on our products and services. Email: worldmarketing@focalpress.com – we want to hear your views!

Membership is FREE. To join, visit our website and register. If you require any further information regarding the on-line club please contact:

Emma Hales, Marketing Manager
Email: emma.hales@repp.co.uk
Tel: +44 (0) 1865 314556
Fax: +44 (0)1865 315472
Address: Focal Press, Linacre House,
Jordan Hill, Oxford, UK, OX2 8DP

Catalogue

For information on all Focal Press titles, our full catalogue is available online at www.focalpress.com and all titles can be purchased here via secure online ordering, or contact us for a free printed version:

USA
Email: christine.degon@bhusa.com

Europe and rest of world
Email: jo.coleman@repp.co.uk
Tel: +44 (0)1865 314220

Potential authors

If you have an idea for a book, please get in touch:

USA
Lilly Roberts, Editorial Assistant
Email: lilly.roberts@bhusa.com
Tel: +1 781 904 2639
Fax: +1 781 904 2640

Europe and rest of world
Christina Donaldson, Editorial Assistant
Email: christina.donaldson@repp.co.uk
Tel: +44 (0)1865 314027
Fax: +44 (0)1865 314572